TIME *to* *Dance*

Weekly Devotional for Dancers

ALYSSA CAMPBELL

ISBN: 1495210987
ISBN-13: 978-1495210983

TABLE OF CONTENTS

WHY SHOULD YOU DANCE?

DANCE AND GOD'S CHARACTER

WHAT DOES DANCE MEAN?

WHAT IS THE PURPOSE?

ALL DANCE CAN GLORIFY GOD

UPKEEP OF A CHRISTIAN DANCER

BIBLICAL EXAMPLES

DANCE AND THE HISTORY OF THE CHURCH

DANCE AND EVANGELISM

WHY SHOULD YOU DANCE?

Week 1

Dance Was Created by God

Read It

Before examining the dimensions of Christian dance, it is important to understand the origins of dance and the evidence for its relevance in scripture. The following scriptures guide you through the truth that dance was created by God for the purpose of bringing him glory.

> _Colossians 1:16_ – _For by him all things were created, in heaven and on earth, visible and invisible, whether thrones or dominions or rulers or authorities – all things were created through him and for him._

The key phrase to note in this scripture is all things. When God created earth and everything in it, he was the only creator. With this logic and scripture proof it can be understood that everything that exists on earth now, as it always has, was created by God and for God. Nothing was originally created with a corrupt purpose. This includes dance as well as any form of worship.

> _Revelation 4:11_ – _Worthy are you, our Lord and God, to receive glory and honor and power, for you created all things, and by your will they existed and were created._

God's omnipotence in creation is a demonstration of how extraordinary he really is. This immense display of power is a reason to glorify him. Nothing can be in existence without his approval. You are in existence and so is dance.

> *Isaiah 43:6-7 – I will say to the north, Give up, and to the south, Do not withhold; bring my sons from afar and my daughters from the end of the earth, everyone who is called by my name, whom I created for my glory, whom I formed and made.*

According to this verse, everyone whom God made was created for God's glory. God has not only created everything, which is a reason to glorify him, but he has also designated from where the glory comes: his people.

> *1 Corinthians 6:20 – Glorify God in your body.*

This scripture is in the section that refers to your body being a temple, making a point at glorifying God through keeping your body pure. Dance is also a way to glorify God with your body and purity in your body is an important part of glorifying God with dance.

Through these four scriptures you can get a brief understanding of the magnitude of creation and why you must glorify God. Since God created everything and dance is part of that, you can conclude that dance is a God-given way to glorify him.

Learn It

How does God's display of power in creation change the way you feel about dance?

Is there any kind of dance that you feel does not bring glory to God? Why?

What can you do to remind yourself of the origins of dance and its purpose of bringing God glory?

Live It

During your warm-up, think about how powerful and brilliant God is. Remember that God created dance for the purpose of bring him glory. Allow that to affect both your attitude and movement while you warm-up. Use this time not only to warm-up your body but also to warm-up your heart. Keeping these things in mind may cause you to dance fuller, focus more, and be more expressive.

Week 2

Dance Brings Joy to God

Read It

Too often Christians make their faith about finding their own joy. The tendency is to forget that the only reason Christians can experience joy is because God did first. Joy is reciprocal. He delights in his people and in all he created. This gives a reason to be joyful and to delight in him. Obedience and worship then stirs up joy in God's heart.

> *Colossians 3:17* – *And whatever you do, in word or deed, do everything in the name of the Lord Jesus, giving thanks to God the Father through him.*

The most important piece to bringing God joy is the heart of your actions. In all that you do you must keep your focus on God. This focus makes the actions intentional, meant for the glory of God alone. The position of your heart is the foundation of your worship.

> *Psalm 149:3-4* – *Let them praise his name with dancing, making melody to him with tambourine and lyre! For the Lord takes pleasure in his people; he adorns the humble with salvation.*

Throughout the Psalms you are commanded to worship God in various forms. As you learned in the previous study, worship was created by God and God delights in his creation. In this verse you see that dance is a form of worship that gives God pleasure.

> *Zephaniah 3:17* – *The Lord your God is in your midst, a mighty one who will save; he will rejoice over you with gladness; he will quiet you by his love; he will exult over you with loud singing.*

God takes so much joy in his people, whose hearts are truly focused on him, that he sings over us. Why not respond to God's singing for you with your dancing for him?

In order to bring joy to a God who has everything, your worship must be intentional. The gift of dance came from God and when you use it intentionally for its original purpose that brings joy to God. He even provides the music!

Learn It

Identify some things that turn your focus in dance away from God. How can you overcome these?

What are some ways that you express joy? How can you incorporate these into worship?

Bringing joy to a God who needs nothing seems like a challenge. What can you do in your personal or dance life that will make God joyful?

Live It

Think of three common movements that express joy (jumping, clapping, etc.). Use these as a basis to create an 8-count dance phrase (or longer) that expresses your joy to God.

Imagine that all of the songs used during rehearsal today are God's voice singing and rejoicing over you. Allow the thought of his presence and joy to guide the emotion and focus behind your movement.

Week 3

Dance is a Sacrifice to God

Read It

To sacrifice is to surrender something you possess (whether it is an object or a personal gift) that holds value to you in order to benefit or serve something or someone else. Sacrifice in scripture is often associated with the blood and food sacrifices of the Old Testament, but the following verses show how your praise and worship in whatever form is also a pleasing sacrifice to God.

> *Romans 12:1 – I appeal to you therefore, brothers, by the mercies of God, to present your bodies as a living sacrifice, holy and acceptable to God.*

Just as Jesus offered his body as a sacrifice for us, so you should offer yours for him. However, Christ took death for you on the cross which means that your sacrifice must be in how you live ("a living sacrifice"). If God has given you a gift that is carried out with your body, the only way to properly use your gift is to offer it back only to the one who gave it.

> *Hebrews 13:15 – Through him then let us continually offer up a sacrifice of praise to God, that is, the fruit of the lips that acknowledge his name.*

In this verse you are told to continually offer praise. If you are not using the gifts God has given you to praise Him, you are not following His will. The word 'continually' signifies that there will be other things you will have to give up in order to offer your sacrifice of praise as often as you should. Praise is not optional. It is continual.

> *Psalm 107:22 – And let them offer sacrifices of thanksgiving, and tell of his deeds in songs of joy!*

Thanksgiving is also a sacrifice to God. It is the acknowledgement that you are not capable of providing for yourself. There are many ways to give thanks to God, including dance and song. A big part of using your gift properly is showing thanks. Giving thanks keeps your focus on God as well as sacrificing the credit for your gift. Only God can provide.

> *But I must confess that there are days when my circumstances don't seem to lend themselves to worship. Days when I feel so caught up in my own problems or so pulled down by my own depression that entering into worship would almost feel hypocritical. What am I to do on those days? - On those days I am to worship anyway! I am to bring the Lord what the Bible calls sacrificial praise: 'So through Jesus let us always offer to God our sacrifice of praise, coming from lips that speak His name.'(Hebrews 13:15)*
> *-Claire Cloninger*

Learn It

What are some ways to offer your gift of dance back to God besides performing?

What have you sacrificed in order to have more time to praise God with the gift He has given you? How has this changed the way you praise Him?

When someone compliments you on your gift/talent, what is your immediate response? Do you take the credit for your own hard work or do you sacrifice it and give it all to the glory of God?

Live It

Make a sacrifice this week: Take one hour a day out of
the time you normally spend watching TV, playing video
games, etc. and use that time to work on the gift God has
given you. Praise him through it.

Week 4

Dance is Prayer

Read It

Prayer is communication with God. Whether it is a request, thanksgiving, praise, or confession, prayer directly connects you to the God who created you. When you come to God in prayer you are speaking from your heart and it is nearly impossible to express the heart without showing it in the body. The examples below demonstrate how important it is to pray using your entire selves, not just your words.

> *Psalm 141:2 – May my prayer be set before you like incense; may the lifting up of my hands be like the evening sacrifice.*

Prayer is pleasing to God. He wants you to communicate with him and he takes joy in your desire to do so. Lifting of hands is a simple gesture that speaks volumes and is often used to portray offering something to God or accepting a gift from God, as well as many other emotions. Using gestures in prayer is indicative of an abundance of emotion that cannot be suppressed. Express it.

> *Daniel 9:3 – So I turned to the Lord God and pleaded with him in prayer and petition, in fasting, and in sackcloth and ashes.*

In the Old Testament, a sign of mourning or repentance

was the way that someone was dressed. They would remove their normal clothing and wear sackcloth (a course fabric made from goat's hair). Then they would sprinkle ashes over their heads, signifying insignificance or worthlessness, that they felt lower than the dust on the ground. These very vivid external representations of emotions were a proclamation of a spiritual attitude. This behavior was a way to connect the external, bodily self to the spiritual, prayerful self. Showing the emotions externally made the conviction more real internally.

> *Psalm 84:2 – My soul longs, yes, faints for the courts of the Lord; my heart and flesh sing for joy to the living God.*

This verse fully demonstrates how the heart and body are inseparable. The soul faints, taking on a physical action, while the flesh cries out, an emotional reaction. What is felt in the heart is expressed in the body.

> *Good art is a form of prayer. It's a way to say what is not sayable.*
> *-Frederich Busch*

Learn It

What are some common gestures you use to express your emotions? Could you communicate those same emotions without using the gestures?

When you speak to a friend do you use your hands, facial expressions, or movements to help you make your point? Do you talk to God the same way?

Live It

As you pray this week allow God to see your heart as well
as hear it. Do what comes naturally, whether it is simply
lifting your hands or changing your posture or whether
you feel like dancing your prayer instead of speaking it.
Notice whether the use of your whole body makes your
prayer feel more intimate with God.

Week 5

Dance Connects the Body of Christ

Read It

Worship is giving God the best that He has given you. Be careful what you do with the best you have. Whenever you get a blessing from God, give it back to Him as a love gift. Take time to meditate before God and offer the blessing back to Him in a deliberate act of worship. If you hoard a thing for yourself, it will turn into spiritual dry rot, as the manna did when it was hoarded. God will never let you hold a spiritual thing for yourself; it has to be given back to Him that He may make it a blessing to others.
- Oswald Chambers

The greatest purpose of a gift from God is to glorify God. The second greatest purpose is to bless others. Anyone who sees you dance for the glory of God or knows your heart in your actions will be blessed by you in some way. By giving your gift first to God, then to others, you are connecting yourself to everyone who is blessed by your actions.

1 Corinthians 12:12 – For just as the body is one and has many members, and all the members of the body, though many, are one body, so it is with Christ.

According to this scripture, anyone who is in a relationship with God is a member of the body of Christ. You are already connected to other Christians all over the world and you come into a deeper connection through fellowship and worship. Not everyone has the same gifts or worships in the same way, so dancers, singers, musicians, teachers, preachers, prayers, etc. are all required to bring the body of Christ into a complete worship experience.

> _Psalm 86:9_ – _All the nations you have made shall come and worship before you, O Lord, and shall glorify your name._

Worship will bring every Christian from every nation together in unity to glorify God. Worship happens all the time all over the world in many different expressions. Dance is one of those expressions and is and will be a part of this global worship experience.

The connection of the body of Christ happens in several ways. Dance plays a part in this connection by blessing everyone involved in the worship experience as well as being part of a global experience. The idea of this global experience is that at any point in time there are people worshipping God somewhere on earth. Even when you are not in an intentional state of worship, somewhere someone else is.

Learn It

Have you ever been in a place of worship and felt like the song, message, drama, or dance was intended just for you? How did that make you feel?

Do you have difficulty remembering that you are connected to and should be in unity with other Christians? What can you do to remind yourself and act accordingly?

Does knowing that you are part of an ongoing global worship experience change how you worship?

Live It

As you dance this week, remember that people on the other side of the world are worshipping too. Participate in worshipping God with them.

Learn about the needs or burdens of someone this week (maybe a friend or even a stranger). Pray for them through dance. You may choose to video tape it and show that person, but even if you don't, your prayers will still be a blessing to them.

Week 6

Dance will be Present in Heaven

Read It

This earthly body is slow and heavy in all its motions, listless and soon tired with action. But our heavenly bodies shall be as fire; as active and nimble as our thoughts are.
-John Wesley

Philippians 3:20-21: But our citizenship is in heaven, and from it we await a Savior, the Lord Jesus Christ, who will transform our lowly body to be like his glorious body, by the power that enables him even to subject all things to himself.

In Heaven, your bodies will be transformed into a new heavenly body. This body will be capable of much more than you ever could have anticipated here on earth. With these new bodies you will be able to more fully worship a God of indescribable glory.

1 Corinthians 15:35-38: But someone will ask, "How are the dead raised? With what kind of body do they come?" You foolish person! What you sow does not come to life unless it dies. And what you sow is not the body that is to be, but a bare kernel, perhaps of wheat or of some other grain. But God gives it a body as he has chosen, and to each kind of seed its own body.

In these verses Paul explains that your bodies on earth are like the seeds that God has sown here. You have not even come close to reaching your full potential and these bodies must die, just like a seed dies, to produce the life that you are created for. Since you know that you were created to worship and glorify God, how much more enthusiastic and brilliant will that worship be when your bodies can reach their full spiritual potential?

> *Revelation 7:9-12:* *After this I looked, and behold, a great multitude that no one could number, from every nation, from all tribes and peoples and languages, standing before the throne and before the Lamb, clothed in white robes, with palm branches in their hands, and crying out with a loud voice, "Salvation belongs to our God who sits on the throne, and to the Lamb!" And all the angels were standing around the throne and around the elders and the four living creatures, and they fell on their faces before the throne and worshiped God, saying, "Amen! Blessing and glory and wisdom and thanksgiving and honor and power and might be to our God forever and ever! Amen."*

In Heaven, you have the honor of coming together with all believers, angels, heavenly elders, and heavenly creatures in unity to worship God. Worship in Heaven will consist of every kind of worship possible always being done to the maximum potential.

Learn It

How much thought have you put into what Heaven will be like? What expectations do you have for the spiritual, emotional, and physical aspects of Heaven?

Think of the greatest athletes you have ever seen. Now imagine having greater abilities than all of them combined and never getting tired. What would you do with that kind of ability?

Live It

Think of the greatest athlete you have ever seen and be reminded of the fact that you are not even close to your full potential. Your ultimate life is in Heaven, praising God with your new heavenly body that is in no way inhibited by earthly boundaries. Imagine what that will be like and praise God as if you had no boundaries.

Try to worship God in a new way this week. Step outside of the boundaries you have put on yourself as a reminder that in Heaven there are no limits on your ability to worship.

DANCE

AND

GOD'S

CHARACTER

Week 7

Devotion

Read It

Devotion is defined as profound dedication. It is also a way to worship God. Devotion to God keeps your eyes fixed on Him and His will for your lives. It is not only something that you are required to do, but it is part of God's character that he demonstrated for you first.

> _Deuteronomy 31:6_ – _He will not leave you or forsake you._

This phrase is spoken many times over throughout scriptures, most often before a time that will greatly test and challenge the person who hears these words. It is meant to be a comfort and reassurance. It is a reminder that God's love goes beyond circumstance or personal action. Your relationship with God is not based on what you can do or give. God has already promised to never leave you. That kind of devotion and love encourages the same from you.

> _Matthew 28: 20_ – _And behold, I am with you always, to the end of the age._

Again, this verse reiterates what was said in Deuteronomy. God is with you always. Once you have genuinely accepted Him you cannot get rid of Him! That is how much he loves you and cares about you. He is profoundly dedicated to you to the end of the age.

1 Thessalonians 5:16-18 – Rejoice always, pray without ceasing, give thanks in all circumstances; for this is the will of God in Christ Jesus for you.

This verse is a call to reflect the devotion that God has shown you. His love is constant and He never leaves you, therefore, you should rejoice in Him constantly and have Him always in your hearts and minds. If you live your lives with this kind of devotion, everything you do becomes praise and worship.

Learn It

Have you ever felt like God was not with you? What reminded you that he will never leave?

What helps you stay constant in your devotion to God? What distracts you from it?

Live It

Find something this week that will help you remember to be devoted God all the time (wear a Jesus bracelet, keep your Bible with you, only listen to Christian music, etc.). See how that changes your attitude and worship.

Week 8

Humility

Read It

It is easy to lose sight of humility in the performing arts. Doing anything in front of an audience is a set up for pride to creep in and take the spotlight. The greatest example of failed humility in scripture is Lucifer. Lucifer was the angel whose pride caused him to be cast out of Heaven and forevermore known as Satan. Scripture describing Lucifer (Isaiah 14 and Ezekiel 28)[1] illustrates a guardian cherub who was the worship leader of the heavenly hosts. The name Lucifer has roots in the Hebrew word 'halel' which means 'to praise.' Lucifer's job was to lead heaven in glorifying God, but Lucifer coveted God's glory. As someone whose job was to use the arts to glorify God, Lucifer is a prime example of how careful artists need to be when facing the opportunity for glory and fame.

Ezekiel 28:17 – Your heart was proud because of your beauty; you corrupted your wisdom for the sake of your

---

[1] Isaiah 14 and Ezekiel 28 are passages of scripture that are directed toward the king of Babylon and the king of Tyre, however, language such as "you were in Eden," "you were an anointed guardian cherub," and "you are fallen from heaven" lead to the conclusion that these passages may be figuratively speaking of the fall of Lucifer as well as a direct warning to these kings.

splendor. I cast you to the ground; I exposed you before kings, to feast their eyes on you.

This verse describes the pride that was in Lucifer's heart. Notice that Lucifer still has his beauty and wisdom, but his pride corrupted it. The result of pride is fall. Because Lucifer ignored his call to bring God glory and focused on his own glory, he was cast down and exposed. Humility is not an option. God does not share his glory with anyone. You either come before God in humility or God will make you humble.

1 Peter 5:6 – Humble yourselves, therefore, under the mighty hand of God so that at the proper time he may exalt you.

God calls you to be a humble people. The purpose of your lives is to bring God glory; to point the way to Him. If you allow yourselves to get in the way of that purpose you are corrupting the wisdom and gifts that God has given you and damaging the purpose and opportunity that God has put in your lives. But if you are obedient and live in humility, giving God glory, your reward is in Heaven.

Philippians 2:8 – And being found in human form, he humbled himself by becoming obedient to the point of death, even death on a cross.

Jesus is an example of perfect humility. He left His paradise in Heaven to become a servant of the world. He left His place of perfection and glory to die a cruel and painful death for you. He came from peace and beauty to take on your sin; to cleanse you and save you. He became the lowest of lows so that you could be raised up with Him and experience the fullness of His glory in Heaven with Him.

Learn It

Do you ever struggle with pride? In what areas of your life are you easily prideful?

Is there someone in your life that is a good example of humility? Describe him/her.

In moments of pride, what can you do to remind yourself of the example of Jesus' humility?

Live It

As you perform this week (this could be anything: dance, singing, giving a presentation at school or work, etc) imagine that God is the only person in your audience. Make the necessary changes to be sure that your performance or presentation impresses God. He is your most important audience.

Week 9

Wisdom

Read It

In order to share any gift that God has given you, you must first be knowledgeable of how and why it is to be used. It would be impossible to dance about the grace of God or about the law of God if you do not understand or have not experienced these concepts. When you use the gift of dance to present an idea or story from scripture, you are also acknowledging that you have sought after and received the wisdom pertaining to that idea.

> *James 1:5 – If any of you lacks wisdom, let him ask God, who gives generously to all without reproach, and it will be given him.*

Wisdom is a gift that God gives you. It is something you must desire and seek and if you come to God with that desire he will graciously provide.

> *Proverbs 9:10 – The fear of the Lord is the beginning of wisdom, and the knowledge of the Holy One is insight.*

In order to receive the wisdom that God so generously provides, you must first fear the Lord. If you have not accepted God into your heart as your Lord and Savior, your heart is not open to the wisdom that comes with new life. Another part of wisdom laid out in this scripture is knowledge. Knowledge can only be obtained through study. In order to prepare your heart and mind for the wisdom of God, you must study scripture and know it well.

> *James 3:13 – Who is wise and understanding among you? By his good conduct let him show his works in the meekness of wisdom.*

This verse is a call to let wisdom shine through your works. If you truly understand scripture as a whole as well as the specific subjects behind your dance, it will shine through. Wisdom is not boastful, but is demonstrated in meekness and humility. As you learned in the previous study, humility is a necessary characteristic for artists and it is even more necessary with the gift of wisdom.

Learn It

How often do you read your Bible? Are you simply reading it or are you studying it and learning it?

When you perform, how intently do you study the scripture and subjects related to your performance?

Have you asked God to guide you and give you wisdom?

Live It

Read your Bible everyday this week. Challenge yourself to talk to someone about what you read so you will learn the scripture rather than just read it.

If you are leading worship or worshiping on your own, ask God to give you wisdom about what you are doing first. Pray about the subject and see what you can find in scripture to guide your worship.

Week 10

Faithfulness

Read It

Just like you are not saved by good works, but by faith which produces good works, so also your ministry is not based on your technique and skill, but your faith which shines through your movement. Faithfulness is required of followers of Christ and is therefore required of those who lead or participate in worship.

> *Psalm 89:5 – Let the heavens praise your wonders, O Lord, your faithfulness in the assembly of the holy ones!*

God is the perfect image of faithfulness. There are countless stories and references to how faithful God is throughout scripture. No matter what you do or say, God is faithful to love you and save you. His faithfulness is a reason to praise Him.

> *1 Corinthians 4:2 – Moreover, it is required of stewards that they be found faithful.*

A steward is someone who manages something for another person. As artists, you are stewards of worship for God. You manage this gift and therefore must be faithful to its purpose. To use dance for your own gain or to benefit someone or something else is unfaithful to God, who provided this gift to be used for His glory.

> *Proverbs 3:3 – Let not steadfast love and faithfulness forsake*

you; bind them around your neck; write them on the tablet of your heart.

You are to be bound to Christ in faithfulness. This scripture tells you to always be faithful in your heart as well as to show your faithfulness openly (bound around your neck). One way to demonstrate your faithfulness to God is to use your gifts only for Him. Whenever you dance, let it be a symbol of your faithfulness. Use it for no other purpose than to glorify God.

Faithfulness is a mark of a true servant of God. Temptations that can pull your attention away from your true purpose are everywhere. It is easy to stray from faithfulness, but if your heart is steadfast and you are faithful to God's purpose, people will see God being glorified through your gifts.

Learn It

How has God been faithful to you?

How can you praise God for His faithfulness?

In what ways can dance demonstrate faithfulness?

Live It

Read a story about faithfulness this week (Hosea is a good example of God's faithfulness to His people. Job is a great model of faithfulness to God.). Dedicate your time of reading and study to God. Worship Him in faithfulness through dance, continuing to meditate on the scripture you read.

Love

Read It

People show love in new ways every day. In dance, there are also many ways to show the love of God. You can demonstrate it as a theme in a dance, you can show God's love by being obedient and listening to your instructor, you can show love through teaching, you can love the congregation by leading them in a new way to worship God. Whatever you do can be done in love if you allow love to rule your heart and your actions.

> *Ephesians 5:2 – And walk in love, as Christ loved us and gave himself up for us, a fragrant offering and sacrifice to God.*

You are meant to model your life after the example of Christ's love. He sacrificed the most that He could, Himself, for the salvation of believers. As a Christian, it is your calling to sacrifice your life in love to Christ. Everything you do in love will reflect the love that He showed when He died on the cross.

> *1 Timothy 1:5 – The aim of our charge is love that issues from a pure heart and a good conscience and a sincere faith.*

God's love is not forced. It results from the purity of God's heart and intentions. Your love should be likewise.

You should be so rooted in your faith and devoted to a pure heart and mind that love flows from you naturally. If you find it difficult to be an example of love you may need to check your walk with God.

> *Hebrews 6:10 – For God is not unjust so as to overlook your work and the love that you have shown for his name in serving the saints, as you still do.*

Dance is a form of service. To serve someone is to meet their needs at the expense of your own time and effort. As a dancer, you serve by leading your audience into a worship experience. As a dance teacher, you serve your students by helping them grow in the gift God has given them. As a choreographer, you serve by allowing God to use you to express an idea or theme based in scripture. Acts of service are acts of love and God looks favorably on them.

Love is not always easy to express, but as long as you stay focused on God, studying scripture, and working toward purity, love will pour out of you effortlessly. In many ways, it is easier to show love through a gift that God has given you than through intentional acts of love. God gave you individual gifts so that love could be accomplished in infinite ways. Showing love through dance may come more naturally to you than showing love through words or action and that is exactly how God created you.

Learn It

Do you ever find it difficult to show love? What do you think is the cause of that?

How can you show love through dance in a practical way?

Do you know someone who is a great example of consistent love in your life? Why do you think love flows naturally from that person?

Live It

Before you dance this week, prepare your heart. Make sure you are focused on God and are committed to purity. Read a couple of verses about God's love before each warm up or dance and think about expressing that as you move.

Week 12

Unity

Read It

You have already learned about how dance connects the body of Christ and promotes unity among believers, but dance should also reflect a different kind of unity. You are made of a soul, body, and spirit just as God is made up of the Father, Son, and Holy Spirit. Just like the trinity, your three parts must be in unity in order to fulfill your purpose.

> *2 Corinthians 13:14 – The grace of the Lord Jesus Christ and the love of God and the fellowship of the Holy Spirit be with you all.*

Throughout scripture there are references to the three parts that make up the trinity. Here they are all together, showing their separate purposes while being present in one God. The parts that make up the trinity Godhead are reflected in you. God created mankind in His image (Gen. 1:26-27), including his triune characteristic. Jesus, the Son of God, came to earth as a man, a physical form with a body. God the Father is the creator. He is the giver of life. The Holy Spirit is God's presence around and within us. It is the power and guidance in our lives which gives us knowledge and wisdom.

1 Thessalonians 5:23 – Now may the God of peace himself sanctify you completely, and may your whole spirit and soul and body be kept blameless at the coming of our Lord Jesus Christ.

This scripture describes the three parts of a person that mirror the trinity. These three parts are the spirit, soul, and body. The Greek word for spirit refers to intellect and reason. The spirit is the part of you that has a conscience and a sense of responsibility and rationality. It is the decision making part of you. The soul comes from the Greek word which refers to the life which animates the physical body. It is the source of desire and emotion and the part of you that has personality. The body is your physical form and vessel that contains your spirit and soul. Without the other two your body would be inanimate. These three parts are called to be "blameless," which can only happen if all three are in accordance with one purpose – to be pure and holy.

Deuteronomy 6:4-5 – Hear, O Israel: The Lord our God, the Lord is one. You shall love the Lord your God with all your heart and with all your soul and with all your might.

The Old Testament used slightly different words for the triune division. Here, heart coincides with spirit, soul is still soul, and might refers to the body (your physical effort). In this verse all three parts are called to love God completely, being one with each other in the desires of life.

It is very important to have this unity within the triune characteristics of yourself. You must give all of yourself to fully engage in the gifts God has given you.

Learn It

Give some examples of how you could dance without the unity of your spirit, soul, and body. How would this effect what you are doing?

What can you do prior to a dance class or performance to make sure your spirit, soul, and body are in unity?

Live It

Try to focus this week on staying in unity in all that you do. Before you make a big decision or do anything in front of anyone or even read your Bible on your own, ask yourself a few questions. What is the purpose of doing this? Do I really want to do this? Am I doing this for my benefit or for God's glory? Does my attitude reflect my desire?

Make a checklist of questions to ask yourself to make sure that your spirit, soul, and body are completely engaged in unity in what you are doing.

WHAT DOES DANCE MEAN?

Week 13

Dictionary Definition

Read It

Everyone has their own idea of dance. Whether you have very little exposure or have been dancing your whole life, you could probably come up with your own definition and you will always be right in some sense. The meaning of dance has changed since its creation. In order to get back to the original and pure definition, you will first have to understand what dance means now. Below are several definitions of dance from current dictionaries.

> *Merriam Webster Dictionary[2]: A series of rhythmic and patterned bodily movements usually performed to music.*

> *Oxford Dictionary[3]: Move rhythmically to music, typically following a set sequence of steps.*

> *Cambridge Dictionary[4]: To move the body and feet in rhythm to music.*

In each of these definitions, dance has been stripped down to the basics. It uses movement, rhythm, and music. To non-dancers, these definitions may seem perfectly appropriate, but to dancers the meaning is completely different.

---

[2] *Merriam-Webster's Collegiate Dictionary*, 11th Edition, s.v. "dance."
[3] *New Oxford American Dictionary*, 3rd Edition, s.v. "dance."
[4] *Cambridge Advanced Learner's Dictionary*, 3rd Edition, s.v. "dance."

Below are several definitions of dance from dancers and choreographers.

> *Martha Graham: Dance is the hidden language of the soul.*

> *John Dryden: Dance is the poetry of the foot.*

> *Ruth St. Denis: I see dance being used as communication between body and soul, to express what is too deep, too fine for words.*

The differences between these definitions and the dictionary definitions are quite obvious. While the dictionaries refer to quantitative, measurable aspects of dance, the dancers and choreographers see dance as a deeper and more poetic art. They use dance to communicate and to express. Nowhere in these definitions is there any mention of music or rhythm. While that is part of dance, it may not be the most important part.

These definitions are an example of the stark contrast in how dance is viewed by different people. With this much variance in one word, it is important to search the origins of dance to get back to its original definition and purpose.

Learn It

How do you define dance?

Why do you think there are so many different definitions of dance?

Live It

As you dance this week think about what you are doing. How would you define your actions, emotions, and thoughts while dancing? Write it down and create a definition that captures the entire experience of dance.

Week 14

Biblical Definition

Read It

Since you know that dance was created by God, the only place to look for the original purpose and definition of dance is scripture. While there is no "dance is…" verse in the Bible, there are many scripture references to dance providing glimpses of its purpose and function.

Jeremiah 31:4 – Again I will build you, and you shall be built, O virgin Israel! Again you shall adorn yourself with tambourines and shall go forth in the dance of the merrymakers.

Dance is a symbol of renewal and a sign of celebration. Dance was used in many places throughout scripture to celebrate. It was commonly used at the return of victorious battles, at weddings, and at other feasts and celebrations (such as the return of the prodigal son).

Psalm 30:11-12 – You have turned for me my mourning into dancing; you loosed my sackcloth and clothed me with gladness, that my glory may sing your praise and not be silent. O Lord my God, I will give thanks to you forever!

Dance is an expression of emotion. Here, dance is an expression of joy. There are also examples of dance or movement expressing sorrow, grief, love, and thanksgiving. The Psalms contain many references to emotion overflowing into movement.

> _Psalm 149:3 – Let them praise his name with dancing, making melody to him with tambourine and lyre!_

Dance is a way to praise and communicate with God. The biggest difference between scriptural definitions of dance and the definitions you learned from dictionaries and dancers is that dance in scripture is always directed toward God. Dance is not fulfilling its purpose unless it is intended only for the glory of God.

From the instances of dance found throughout scripture, the Biblical definition of dance would be something like this:

Dance was created by God to be used by His people as a physical representation of events, emotions, and prayer to bring glory to Him alone.

Learn It

What function does dance most often have in your life?

Do you find that you dance differently if you are intentional about dancing for God alone?

How can you change the perception of dance for people around you?

Live It

Do an improvisation warm up and try praying through your movement. Allow your thoughts and prayers to guide what you do.

Week 15

Hebrew Words

Read It

If we get our information from the biblical material there is no doubt that the Christian life is a dancing, leaping, daring life.
– Eugene Peterson

Looking into the meanings behind the original Hebrew and Greek words in scripture can shed light on a deeper definition of Biblical dance. It is easy to search for the word 'dance' in scripture, and you will find a fair amount of verses if you do so, but there are many instances throughout the Bible in which a word of emotion or celebration is used, but the Hebrew for that word can also mean to leap, turn, or dance. Dance is present but hidden in hundreds of places in scripture. Here are some Hebrew words that can be found in the Old Testament.

> *Chuwl – whirl, dance, writhe, twist. This word is used to mean 'dance' in Judges 21:21 and 23 but it is also used for 'writhe in pain' throughout Isaiah and 'wait anxiously' in Job.*

This indicates the strong connection between movement and emotion throughout scripture.

Mecholah – a dance. This Hebrew word for dance is used after a victory (Judges 11, 1 Samuel 18, 2 Samuel 21), as an act of praise (Exodus 15), as well as in idolatrous worship (Exodus 32).

This word is the general term for dance and so is used in both holy and unholy examples.

Chagag – celebrate, dancing, keeping festival, to move in a circle, to march in a sacred procession. This word is typically used to describe the keeping of a festival or a celebration. It can be seen in Exodus 12: 14, Deuteronomy 16:15, 1 Samuel 30:16, Leviticus 23:39 and many other places throughout the Old Testament.

In each of these verses the word is used to acknowledge a celebration. The Hebrew definition suggests that a major part of these celebrations and festivals was dancing.

These definitions give a clearer idea of how important and integrated dance was in the lives of Old Testament believers.

Learn It

What was the last celebration you attended? How important was dance to that celebration?

When you see people expressing emotion or celebrating an event, what common movements do you notice?

When you think of the following words, what is the first image that comes to your mind? Would you consider it dance?

Celebration, joy, pain, sorrow

Live It

Choreograph a four 8-count phrase expressing whatever emotion you feel today. Use intentional movements as well as movements you would express naturally in a conversation or in prayer. Use this to tell God how you feel.

Week 16

Greek Words

Read It

The New Testament was written in Greek and also has several different words that mean dance or express movement. The following are just a few.

> *Orcheomai – to dance. This word is the general term for dance in the original Greek. It is only found a few times in the New Testament in the following verses: Matthew 11:17, Matthew 14:6, Mark 6:22, Luke 7:32.*

Like the general term for dance in Hebrew, this word is used both for holy and unholy dance.

> *Choros – a dance, dancing. This word is used in the story of the prodigal son (Luke 15:25).*

The term choros in Greek generally refers to a dance of celebration or merriment.

> *Skirtao – leap for joy, skip, bound. This word is translated as "leap" in each instance in the New Testament. In all of the verses it is an expression of joy (Luke 1:41, 1:44, Luke 6:23).*

As with the Hebrew terms, this Greek word signifies how integral physical expressions of emotion were for early believers. Emotions that were too strong to contain were expressed freely through movement.

Choregeo – to lead a chorus, lead a group of performers, supply everything needed for an event. There are two instances of this word in the New Testament (2 Corinthians 9:10, 1 Peter 4:11).

Both of the verses are referring to God abundantly supplying the needs of His people. As members of a ministry of performers you should abundantly supply your gifts and services to the church.

As these words demonstrate, dance carries significance in many parts of a person's life. It is an expression of emotion, a symbol of celebration, and a gift to be supplied freely.

Learn It

How important is dance to your daily life?

Why do you think it is important to supply your gift freely to the church?

Do you ever find yourself using movement to express an emotion or idea in a regular conversation? What kind of movements do you typically use?

Live It

Find a couple of verses in the New Testament that have some kind of movement, even if it is small (leap, skip, dance, bow, clap, etc). Using the context of the verses and the movements, try to decipher what emotions or ideas were being expressed.

Week 17

Natural Movements

Read It

Movement is an outward expression of an inward emotion. Even the smallest movements can convey a much deeper meaning than words. There are many natural movements throughout scripture that communicate various emotions and states of a person's heart.

> *Lamentations 3:41* – *Let us lift up our hearts and hands to God in heaven.*

When taken in context, the lifting of hands in this verse symbolizes repentance. It is an outward expression of the position of one's heart. Lifting hands can also show supplication, prayer, praise, seeking God, meditation, or receiving from God.

> *Psalm 95:6* – *Oh come, let us worship and bow down; let us kneel before the Lord, our Maker!*

This verse uses two movements, bowing and kneeling. Kneeling is used to express reverence and submission. The word submission has root origins that mean 'to sink' or 'to lower,' which can be carried out by kneeling.

> *Nehemiah 8:6* – *And they bowed their heads and worshiped*

the Lord with their faces on the ground.

Bowing is the act of putting oneself lower than another person. It is a representation of humility and recognition of authority. This verse happens after Ezra reads the Book of the Law of Moses to all who could understand. They recognized from this act that God had authority over them and they demonstrated it by bowing and making themselves as low as possible.

These small movements may not look like dance, but they are what make up dance. They are widely present in dances that are performed to bring glory to God and to portray emotions or themes that are relatable and present in scripture.

Learn It

What are some movements that you use to communicate to God?

Think of two other movements besides the ones described above. What do you think they would mean?

Why do you think movement helps you express and communicate with God? What is the purpose of this kind of communication?

Live It

Pay attention during the worship service this Sunday.
How many different movements do you see and what do
they seem to be communicating?

Week 18

Unholy Dance

Read It

Dance was created for the glory of God. However, since the gift was given to humans it has become corrupted. There are infinite ways to corrupt the gifts that God has given you, but some are more tempting than others. Here are a few examples of how dance has been used for unholy purposes.

> _Exodus 32:19_ – And as soon as he came near the camp and saw the calf and the dancing, Moses' anger burned hot, and he threw the tablets out of his hands and broke them at the foot of the mountain.

The context of this verse is while the Israelites were in the wilderness after escaping Egypt. Moses had been on the mountain receiving the Ten Commandments from God. While he was gone, the people melted their gold and created a golden calf to worship. They prepared a feast and sang and danced around the golden calf, treating it like a god. They used the gifts that God had given them (their gold, their voices, their bodies, their food, etc) and offered them up to a god that was created, not the God who is the Creator. This action resulted in the anger of God and Moses. God put a plague on them as punishment and Moses had to go back up the mountain to get a new set of the commandments.

Matthew 14:6-7 – But when Herod's birthday came, the daughter of Herodias danced before the company and pleased Herod, so that he promised with an oath to give her whatever she might ask.

In this example, dance was used as a tool of persuasion to get what Herodias wanted. Her daughter was able to use her movements to entice King Herod and fulfill her selfish desires. What she asked for was the head of John the Baptist. Her actions directly resulted in the death of the prophet whose purpose was to prepare the world for Christ.

Using your gifts and talents for the wrong purpose can have serious consequences. No matter what you do with your gift, if it is outside of God's purpose it is hurting God and it is hurting you.

Learn It

What are the biggest temptations for you to use your gifts for something other than God's glory?

What are some other ways that dance can be used for unholy purposes?

How can you stay accountable for your reactions to these types of temptations?

Live It

Throughout this next week, be more sensitive to the temptations around you. Notice a common pattern for yourself and find scripture to help keep your thoughts and actions holy in your weakest points.

WHAT

IS

THE

PURPOSE?

Week 19

Praise

Read It

Our entire being is fashioned as an instrument of praise. Just as a master violin maker designs an instrument to produce maximum aesthetic results, so God tailor-made our bodies, souls and spirits to work together in consonance to produce pleasing expressions of praise and worship. When we use body language to express praise, that which is internal becomes visible.
-Don McMinn

The act of praise brings glory to God for things he has done, will do, has brought you through, etc. Even in the face of hardship you can praise God knowing that he thinks you are strong enough to handle what is in front of you. Praise is acknowledging, thanking, and glorifying God for something.

Isaiah 12:5 – Sing praises to the Lord, for he has done gloriously; let this be made known in all the earth.

Praise is not meant to be kept to yourself. Praise is an exclamation that is meant to be seen and heard. It is a declaration of faith to God that he is glorious and holy and has done great things. When people see this in your life they will want to praise with you and find out what is so wonderful.

Psalm 150:4 – Praise him with tambourine and dance; praise him with strings and pipe!

Dancers are instructed to praise with musicians. Praise is not an individual act but a communal act. Complete praise involves more than just the one form you have to offer. Just as we are one body with many parts, praise uses all of those parts to make a beautiful and holy and complete body of praise for God.

Psalm 149:3 – Let them praise his name with dancing, making melody to him with tambourine and lyre!

Again, you are commanded to praise God through dance with musicians. God created dance to be used with other gifts. He intentionally created your gift so that you must share your experience of praise with others in order to fulfill the real purpose.

Praise is meant to bring together the community of God, the body of Christ. We are told throughout scripture to praise God in all circumstances. That may be difficult to do on your own but if you praise God in fellowship, sharing your gifts with others, you will be encouraged and refreshed to continue praising constantly as God designed.

Learn It

What reasons do you have to praise God?

Why is it so important to combine your gifts with the gifts of others to praise God?

How can you use the gift of dance to lead or join praise in a community setting?

Live It

During worship this week, try to use dance in some way. Even if it is just to sway back and forth, maybe bow down or lift your hands. Praise God in reverence and praise him with the musicians and singers who are leading worship. If your church is already accepting of dance, feel free to dance in the aisles. It may change the energy and praise of the people around you also.

Week 20

Worship

Read It

The biggest difference between praise and worship is that praise is glorifying God for something he has done, while worship is glorifying God for who he is. It is the full realization that God is all powerful, all knowing, and always present. He is the Alpha and Omega, he is the savior, the creator, the redeemer. For who he is alone, he deserves unending glory.

> _John 4:24_ – _God is spirit, and those who worship him must worship in spirit and truth._

Since worship is glorifying God simply for who he is, it must be done in complete reverence. Without fully understanding in your heart why you are worshiping, your worship can become stale and staged. This is a time when truth and understanding make your gifts shine for Christ. The position of your heart will be obvious through your body, especially as a dancer.

> _Psalm 95:6_ – _Oh come, let us worship and bow down; let us kneel before the Lord, our Maker!_

Our Lord is our maker. He crafted your body specifically to use it to bring him glory. To do otherwise would be taking his gifts and his craftsmanship for granted. But how beautiful to think that God took the time to decide how many hairs would be on your head, the shape of your nose, how long your legs would be, how big your feet would be. God as creator makes God an intimate part of your life and ministry. Remember this to keep yourself from complaining that "if only I was taller, I could leap higher," or "if I had better balance I could do more turns." Instead remember that God created you "imperfect" so that you could focus on his perfection.

> *Psalm 29:2 – Ascribe to the Lord the glory due his name; worship the Lord in the splendor of holiness.*

Glory is due to God. You owe it to him. No matter what happens in your life, in history, or anywhere in the world; God is who he is. He always has and always will be holy and perfect and virtuous. He will always be your savior. He will always deserve your worship.

Learn It

How do you think dance as worship is different from dance as praise?

Do you think it is necessary to separate these two?

Do you ever find it hard to worship? What reminds you of the reason you worship?

Live It

Write down words that describe who God is. Make
special note of what God has shown you in your life.
Find ways to worship God for these characteristics
through dance. Use any style of dance that works for you
and for the reasons you are worshiping.

Week 21

Expression

Read It

The truest expression of a people is in its dance and in its music. Bodies never lie.
-Agnes de Mille

How people express themselves is the highest indicator of who they are. You can express yourself by what you do, how you do it, what emotions drive you, etc. These qualities are choices you make whether you realize it or not and they show the world (or at least whoever may be watching) who you are. The foods you like, the languages you speak, the type of dance you like; all of these are outward expressions of your inner preferences and desires. Dancers typically find that they have a particular style that they favor and some even have a trademark move. In fact, the only reason dance has become as diverse as it is now is because people were not ashamed to express who they were through the gifts they were given.

Romans 12:6-7 – Having gifts that differ according to the grace given to us, let us use them.

Scripture makes it clear that God has given each person a specific gift that is theirs alone. The body of Christ is made up of every individual and is only complete with all the parts in place. You are called to use your gift. There are no specifics about how to use your gifts except that they are to be used for God's glory. So if you have the gift of dance but you prefer ballet over any other style, use it. Or if you prefer to choreograph, do it. If you know you have been gifted with dance but you also have a gift of teaching, be a dance teacher. If you have been given a gift there is no reason to suppress it or hide from it. It was personally given to you by God. Using your gifts tells the world who you are as an individual in Christ and what your part is in the body of Christ.

> *1 Peter 3:3-4 – Do not let your adorning be external – the braiding of hair and the putting on of gold jewelry, or the clothing you wear – but let your adorning be the hidden person of the heart with the imperishable beauty of a gentle and quiet spirit, which in God's sight is very precious.*

People try to define themselves by what people see. And while your height, eye color, hair color, weight, and other physical features are part of you, they are not you. You are defined by your heart and your spirit. You have a personality and gifts and thoughts that are unique to you. This is how God calls you to define yourself. He even says to adorn yourself with this person. Who you are on the inside should be the first thing people recognize about you. That means you have to show people what you have to offer as an individual.

Learn It

What is the easiest way for you to express yourself?

How can you express both your personality and your faith through dance?

Is it difficult for you to find a balance between expressing who you are in your heart and performing someone else's choreography? Why or why not?

Live It

Write down some things that describe who you are. Use your likes and dislikes, personality traits, emotional traits, describe your faith. Create a short (or long, if you prefer) dance to express who you are. Don't confine yourself to steps, patterns, or movements that you have learned or seen. Allow yourself to create something entirely new and entirely you.

Week 22

Celebration

Read It

*The next time you look in the mirror, just look at the way
the ears rest next to the head; look at the way the hairline
grows; think of all the little bones in your wrist. It is a
miracle. And the dance is a celebration of that miracle.*
– Martha Graham

There is always a reason to celebrate. This morning, you
woke up. That means you are alive. You ate breakfast;
that means God has provided for you. Maybe you went
to school; you are blessed with an education. Or maybe
you went to work; God led you to a job that provides for
you and your family. Throughout scripture, God's
children celebrated. They created feasts and festivals all
throughout the year so they had a calendar packed with
celebration.

> *Luke 15:24-25 – "For this my son was dead, and is alive
> again; he was lost, and is found." And they began to
> celebrate. Now his older son was in the field, and as he came
> and drew near to the house, he heard music and dancing.*

In this story, the son left home to find his own way in the
world. Defeated and with nothing, he returned home
begging only to be a servant with his father's forgiveness.
The father instead celebrated his son's return. Knowing
he was alive was more important than the mistakes he

had made. And how did they celebrate? With music and dancing, of course!

> *2 Samuel 6:21 – And David said to Michal, "It was before the Lord, who chose me above your father and above all his house, to appoint me as prince over Israel, the people of the Lord – and I will celebrate before the Lord."*

King David was celebrating the Ark of the Covenant being brought into Jerusalem. He celebrated with dancing and did so "with all his might" as 2 Samuel states in another verse. His motives are challenged by his wife and he explains that there is nothing that can stop him from celebrating what God has done.

Celebration should be a part of your everyday life. It should not be something rare that only happens at holidays and birthdays. After all, Jesus didn't only take your sins at Easter. He was not born just for Christmas. His purpose was eternal, not annual. You have a reason to celebrate every moment of every day. Do it.

Learn It

What was the last thing you celebrated?

Do you find it hard or easy to celebrate small things?

How can you celebrate even the small things using dance?

Live It

Find something to celebrate everyday this week. Be intentional about celebrating whatever it may be. Do a little dance, sing a song, or tell someone what you are celebrating. Take this week to make yourself more aware of everything God has given you to celebrate.

Week 23

Visualization

Read It

Visualization and metaphor can be found throughout all of scripture. There is a reason for this. We remember things and understand things better if we have a picture of them in our head. The Psalms are filled with metaphors ranging from shepherds to rocks to potters and vases. The New Testament is full of parables, stories that Jesus told so that those listening could understand what he was really saying. These visuals help us grasp a concept that may be out of our reach if it was said in simple terms.

> *Isaiah 45:9 – Woe to him who strives with him who formed him, a pot among earthen pots! Does the clay say to him who forms it, "What are you making?" or "Your work has no handles"?*

This is an example of a metaphor used to make the reader pay attention and think more clearly about what is really behind the words. It is a way of saying "How could you question the authority and decisions of God when you are something he created himself?" God created you just the way he intended. To criticize his work is to question his perfectness. Saying this in a metaphor causes the reader to engage a different part of their brain that sees rather than hears the thought.

John 1:14 – And the Word became flesh and dwelt among us, and we have seen his glory, glory as of the only Son from the Father, full of grace and truth.

Even our savior came in a visible form. Prophecies of the Old Testament spoke of a savior who would come and even when he was here those closest to him still did not understand. They did not understand until they saw. They saw his glory, his sacrifice, his grace, his truth. They saw it in the miracles he performed, how he treated others, his death on the cross, and his resurrection.

Matthew 13:13 – This is why I speak to them in parables, because seeing they do not see, and hearing they do not hear, nor do they understand.

Jesus had to explain to his disciples why he used parables. The people listening would not understand without them. The stories and images are all relatable in the context of the Biblical timeframe. They would understand from their perspective as a farmer or shepherd why the person in the parable would do something. That would then make it easier to understand the bigger and deeper message of the story.

As dancers, God has allowed you to take part in this special privilege. You get to help people understand. Just as stories and metaphors help people see, so does dance. By the movements you perform and stories you dance, you can help an audience understand Biblical truth.

Learn It

How can dance be a visual representation of scriptural truth?

Have you ever understood something better or for the first time after seeing a dance?

Why do you think it is so important for people to have visual representations of scripture?

Live It

Find a piece of scripture that you have a hard time remembering (maybe the Ten Commandments, the Lord's Prayer, the beatitudes, etc.). Try to put movements to each of the parts that you forget. Dance the movements. If you need to see it, try doing it in front of a mirror or recording yourself on video. As you watch it or dance it, does the scripture become easier to remember?

Week 24

Prayer

Read It

Communication is the foundation of all strong relationships. This includes your relationship with God. How else do you know someone but by talking to that person and sharing about yourself? In the same way, dance helps you express yourself and share personal stories and emotions. Dance is a form of communication.

> *Isaiah 26:17 – Like a pregnant woman who writhes and cries out in her pangs when she is near to giving birth, so were we because of you, O Lord.*

It is nearly impossible to be in a huge amount of pain, whether physically, mentally, or spiritually, and not show it externally. It is natural to express what you feel and think with your physical self and makes the expression more clear and powerful. The way you communicate with God is through prayer, so using dance in prayer to God will only enhance your prayer, making it more clear and powerful.

> *Psalm 84:2 – My soul longs, yes, faints for the courts of the Lord; my heart and flesh sing for joy to the living God.*

Using dance in prayer doesn't just show what you are

feeling or thinking, it connects your mind and your heart to your body, making your prayers and petitions stronger by putting your whole self behind the ideas. This scripture shows that connection, including the soul, heart and flesh all in one accord as it sings out for God.

> *2 Chronicles 6:29-30* – *Whatever prayer, whatever plea is made by any man or by all your people Israel, each knowing his own affliction and his own sorrow and stretching out his hands toward this house, then hear from heaven your dwelling place and forgive and render to each whose heart you know, according to all his ways, for you, you only, know the hearts of the children of mankind.*

Prayer is more pure if it comes from your entire self. Using your body to express the desires of your heart and soul make you think more and feel more strongly about what you are asking of or saying to God. God knows what is in your heart, but your actions and sincerity in prayer indicate your heart more clearly.

Learn It

Do you feel more sure of what you say when you use movement with your words?

What do you do when you feel like someone doesn't understand you? Do you speak louder? Add gestures?

Why do you think it is important for your mind, heart, and body to be in one accord in prayer?

Live It

As you pray this week allow yourself to use movement freely and naturally. It doesn't have to be a full dance, but any movement that naturally helps express your thoughts will strengthen your prayer and help you more fully communicate. Take note of whether your prayers feel stronger or more complete with movement.

Week 25

Warfare

Read It

When you think of warfare you probably think of barbaric battles where enemies face off and fire away at each other. This type of warfare is very real, but there is also a spiritual warfare that goes on constantly. It is a battle for the hearts and minds of people. It is a battle between the truths of the gospel and lies. Dance is a part of this kind of warfare. It is a weapon against the enemy.

> *Psalm 149:7-9* - *...to execute vengeance on the nations and punishments on the peoples, to bind their kings with chains and their nobles with fetters of iron, to execute on them the judgment written! This is honor for all his godly ones. Praise the Lord!*

This passage of scripture is entirely filled with ways to praise God before this section. It says to praise God with singing, instruments, and dance and then explains why. Because praising God is truth and the truth will bind up evil and destroy enemies. Praise will execute judgment while bringing honor and glory to God and his people.

> *Psalm 18:33-34* – *He made my feet like the feet of a deer and set me secure on the heights. He trains my hands for war, so*

that my arms can bend a bow of bronze.

This verse demonstrates the importance of preparing a body for physical warfare. The same necessity applies for dance. Since praise is a weapon in spiritual warfare, it is important to train your body to be prepared.

> *Acts 16:25-26 – About midnight Paul and Silas were praying and singing hymns to god, and the prisoners were listening to them, and suddenly there was a great earthquake, so that the foundations of the prison were shaken. And immediately all the doors were opened, and everyone's bonds were unfastened.*

Praising God will destroy the enemy and set you free. Paul and Silas did not let the enemy discourage them. Instead they praised God during a time when they knew the enemy was after them. The result was freedom and victory.

Learn It

Do you think warfare dance should be more personal or public? Why?

How can warfare dance be an encouragement to others?

How can dance help you in your weaknesses (temptations, worries, etc.)?

Live It

Write down one or two things that you struggle with this week. They could be temptations, thinking badly about someone, a task that seems impossible, anything that you need to overcome. Dance it out. Do what you need to do to physically push the devil out of the situation through dance. Praise God in your struggle.

ALL
DANCE
CAN
GLORIFY
GOD

Week 26

Ballet

Read It

Different styles of dance have varying physical and mental requirements. Each type of dance can glorify God in some different way using these physical and mental abilities that make up styles and genres of dance.

Most dancers who become superb ballerinas start training when they are only toddlers. Because ballet is very specific and requires rigorous training to achieve great flexibility and perfect turnout, this type of dance requires devotion and lots of patience. Ballets are usually performed as a production that tells a story (Nutcracker, Swan Lake, etc). Ballet reflects a Christian journey in both the mental and physical training as well as the use of story-telling.

> *Titus 3:14 – And let our people learn to devote themselves to good works, so as to help cases of urgent need, and not be unfruitful.*

Christians are called to be devoted people. Devoting yourself to good works allows you to be a fruitful Christian. Training in ballet requires devotion in order to learn the language of ballet (the French terms, what they mean, what they look like, how to use them in a dance), the positions of ballet, and the time it takes to achieve the ballet body. Learning this kind of devotion does not come easy, but as a dancer you probably have a better grasp on what devotion is and the importance of it.

> *Luke 8:15* – *As for that in the good soil, they are those who, hearing the word, hold it fast in an honest and good heart, and bear fruit with patience.*

Christians are also called to have patience. It is a fruit of the spirit and Christians are told to hold fast to the truth with patience. You can't expect the fruit of your actions to happen immediately, especially where training is concerned. You can't expect to know scripture inside out the moment you become a Christian. You have to study day after day for it to become part of who you are. The same goes in ballet. You can't expect to have perfect turnout the first week you start training. You can't expect to do a full split the first time you try. It takes patience and devotion to train your muscles to move in certain ways, just like it takes patience and devotion to train you heart and mind to live like a Christian.

> *Hebrews 12:10* – *I spoke to the prophets; it was I who multiplied visions, and through the prophets gave parables.*

Parables are all over scripture. They are stories that are told in order to help people understand the message of the gospel. Ballet productions usually tell stories. This form of ballet is one way that ballet can be used to glorify God by touching others. Ballet can be used to tell stories from scripture that help people understand the gospel.

Learn It

Do you find it easier to devote yourself to something you love (such as dance) than to devote yourself to learning scripture?

How can being devoted and patient in dance glorify God?

Why is it important to use ballet to teach others scripture through story-telling?

Live It

Practice some new (or old) ballet steps that you have been learning. Devote yourself to a few that are particularly difficult for you. Write down some of your thoughts as you work through these. Take note of whether you get frustrated, have a breakthrough, learn something new about how you train, etc. Review your notes and remember that being devoted and patient in your faith is the same. It will not be easy and you may get frustrated along the way, but if you keep training and keep working at it, you will see results.

Week 27

Contemporary

Read It

Contemporary dance is not nearly as structured as ballet. There are techniques unique to contemporary dance but overall this style allows more personal freedom than most other dance forms. Contemporary dance gives the dancer a voice and is likely to express some sort of emotion or opinion.

> *Psalm 139:14-16* – *I praise you, for I am fearfully and wonderfully made. Wonderful are your works; my soul knows it very well. My frame was not hidden from you, when I was being made in secret, intricately woven in the depths of the earth. Your eyes saw my unformed substance; in your book were written, every one of them, the days that were formed for me, when as yet there were none of them.*

By allowing your inner self to shine through in dance, you are acknowledging the creator of your being. You are glorifying God when you show people who you are. God created you different from anyone else who ever was or will be. Every dancer has something special to bring and in contemporary dance that is celebrated. Contemporary honors uniqueness that was given to you by God.

2 Corinthians 3:17 – Now the Lord is the Spirit, and where the Spirit of the Lord is, there is freedom.

Contemporary dance allows more freedom than most other forms of dance. This freedom is a way to glorify God because in salvation you find freedom. Using dance to show an audience the freedom you have been given through Christ is a public testimony of his grace and love.

Hebrews 4:15 – For we do not have a high priest who is unable to sympathize with our weaknesses, but one who in every respect has been tempted as we are, yet without sin.

Jesus became entirely human when he was born on earth. He felt the same emotions and struggled with the same temptations and worries as you do. When you dance about your trials and your emotions and freely express yourself, you are connecting with your savior. You are saying that you know you have a God who understands and you can put your faith and trust in him.

Contemporary dance is a free form of dance, allowing you to express who you are, your emotions, your trials, your temptations. This dance form glorifies God in acknowledging how close and intimate he is with you.

Learn It

Do you feel closer to God when you dance about a personal struggle or with a trial or emotion in mind?

How can you express freedom in Christ through contemporary dance?

Is contemporary dance more important for you on a personal or interpersonal level? Why?

Live It

Choose something personal to dance about this week.
Allow yourself to move freely in expression, not confining
yourself to steps you already know. Just be free to
connect with God through movement in your own way.

Week 28

Jazz

Read It

Jazz is typically a flashier, more visually appealing style of dance. The purpose of jazz is to entertain. Because of this, jazz can be a tricky dance style for Christians. It can become difficult to perform jazz without making it about the performer. Jazz does, however, have the components to make a very effective dance for several purposes in Christianity.

> *Psalm 40:3 – He put a new song in my mouth, a song of praise to our God. Many will see and fear, and put their trust in the Lord.*

Since jazz is so high-energy, it is common to do jazz to happy and upbeat music. This makes jazz a great dance form for joyful praise. Joyful praise is praise that can be seen and heard. It has an infectious impact on those who watch and makes others want to join in. Just as this verse demonstrates, people will see this kind of praise and put their trust in the Lord.

> *2 Samuel 6:14 – And David danced before the Lord with all his might.*

Jazz can also be a good dance style for celebration. It usually requires some measure of athleticism and jazz in large groups also tends to be precisely choreographed with a lot of unison. These types of dances are great for places where people celebrate (think of line dances at parties or traditional dances performed at weddings). Jazz is also useful for celebrating on your own. In 2 Samuel David danced with all his might in front of all of Israel.

> _Proverbs 25:28_ – _A man without self-control is like a city broken into and left without walls._

Certain styles of dance produce certain marks of character in dancers. Jazz for Christian dancers develops self-control. While jazz is a fun and visually appealing style, it can also easily lead to temptations of being in the spotlight or dancing too seductively. Those who can perform jazz dances in a Christian setting have developed and demonstrate great self-control.

Learn It

Why is self-control an important character trait for Christians?

What other character qualities can jazz dance teach?

In what situations do you think jazz would be the most appropriate style of dance?

Live It

Create a short jazz combination celebrating something from scripture. Pay attention to the movements you choose and why you choose them. Try to express the joyfulness of the celebration without being too flashy. Make sure the dance is about what you are celebrating and not about you.

Week 29

Hip Hop

Read It

Hip hop is one of the newest styles of dance and because of how fresh and young it is, hip hop serves a great purpose of reaching out to younger audiences. It can be a great tool for evangelism or for connecting a youthful crowd to a higher purpose. Hip hop also takes a good amount of discipline to be able to perform some of the moves, especially break dancing. Being dedicated and disciplined is a character trait that will lead to a faithful and devoted walk with God also.

> *James 1:25 – But the one who looks into the perfect law, the law of liberty, and perseveres, being no hearer who forgets but a doer who acts, he will be blessed in his doing.*

Being a Christian is not just about knowing scripture and what the stories mean. It is about acting on what you know. You must show your faith by your actions and persevere in what you believe. Hip hop is the same way. You can know what hip hop looks like and what it takes to dance it, but until you have actually done it and learned it in your body and not just your head, you will not fully understand or be able to do it. You must be disciplined and devoted to learning this highly stylized form of dance.

> *Romans 10:14-15 – How then will they call on him in*

whom they have not believed? And how are they to believe in him of whom they have never heard? And how are they to hear without someone preaching? And how are they to preach unless they are sent? As it is written, "How beautiful are the feet of those who preach the good news!"

God's word is meant to be heard by everyone. Hip hop reaches a crowd that would be difficult to reach just by preaching or teaching. And how can people know Christ unless someone has been sent to them? Hip hop bridges a gap that allows Christ to be known and character to be taught.

Psalm 45:17 – I will cause your name to be remembered in all generations; therefore nations will praise you forever and ever.

Every generation will know God's name, but every generation cannot be reached the same way. One generation may prefer to listen to traditional sermons and hymns sung with the accompaniment of an organ, but for another generation that may be the very thing that makes the church look unattractive. Hip hop dance is a way to reach out to the younger generations with something new and fresh that tells stories of scripture and encourages learning and growth.

Learn It

Can you think of anyone you know who might respond better to the message of Christ if it was presented through hip hop rather than a traditional church setting? Why do you think this is?

Why do you think discipline is important in hip hop? Why is discipline important for Christians?

Live It

Learn a few hip hop moves this week, whatever your level is try something new. Discipline yourself to practice them until you can do them well. Now do the same with a story or passage of scripture.

Week 30

Fusion

Read It

Fusion dance combines more than one form of dance. It can be done by combining elements from different styles into one string of choreography or by having dancers each perform a different style in one dance. Fusion allows for depth in choreography, showing a range of personal expression and characteristics.

> _Galatians 5:22-23 – But the fruit of the Spirit is love, joy, peace, patience, kindness, goodness, faithfulness, gentleness, self-control; against such things there is no law._

Since each form of dance requires different character traits and displays different qualities, combining multiple dance forms also combines these characteristics, making the dance a greater representation of the dancers as individuals and of the fullness of the fruits of the spirit.

> _Romans 12:5 – So we, though many, are one body in Christ, and individually members of one another._

Fusion presents the different aspects of varying styles of dance in one unique performance, allowing the audience to identify with the style they connect to best as well as the dance as whole. In fusion, the dance is made up of individual styles but it is not complete if it is lacking one. It is a visual representation of what it means to be part of the body of Christ.

> *1 Corinthians 9:22* – *I have become all things to all people, that by all means I might save some.*

Everyone responds to the gospel in different ways and because everyone is different in what catches their interest and what they are willing to listen to, the gospel needs to be presented in ways that will make people see. Because fusion dance is so diverse, there is a dance form that fits the interest of most everyone who watches. This is a big benefit for fusion dance because it catches the interest of a greater audience and allows the message of the dance to be understood by more people.

There are many benefits of combining dance styles besides just being visually appealing. Fusion is a unique representation of the individuality that makes up the wholeness of the body of Christ while being a distinctive platform for reaching an audience with a message of the gospel.

Learn It

What do you think of when you think of the body of Christ? Do you think fusion dance is a good representation of what you see?

What kind of stories or messages do you think would be good for a fusion dance?

Live It

Choose three styles of dance and create a brief dance that uses all three to present an idea or story from scripture. Video tape it or have someone watch it and tell you what they see.

Week 31

Improvisation

Read It

The beautiful thing about improvisation is that it is not planned. It happens quicker than you can think about it and that makes it a projection of your heart rather than a planned outcome. It reveals what is currently driving your spirit at that particular moment. It is a reflection of an intimate experience with God.

> _Romans 8:26_ – _Likewise, the Spirit helps us in our weakness. For we do not know what to pray for as we ought, but the Spirit himself intercedes for us with groaning too deep for words._

Improvisation is a kind of prayer. Sometimes you do not know what to say as you pray, but the Holy Spirit will take over if you allow it. The same happens in improvisation. Allowing the Holy Spirit to take over your body allows you to dance and pray more intimately with God in unity with his Spirit. Removing the thought process behind the dance also removes any inhibitions or prideful motivation. It makes the dance purely about your communication with God.

> _James 4:8_ – _Draw near to God, and he will draw near to you._

Dancing candidly in front of God alone will draw you

closer to him. Improvisation allows you to expose thoughts and emotions that you may not have been able to easily put into words or choreography. It gives an opportunity for you to express what is deeply personal or difficult to convey. When you allow this much of yourself to reach out to God, he will reach back.

> _Matthew 6:6-7_ – _But when you pray, go into your room and shut the door and pray to your Father who is in secret. And your Father who sees in secret will reward you. And when you pray do not heap up empty phrases as the Gentiles do, for they think that they will be heard for their many words._

Improvisation is about the relationship between you and God. He is the only audience you should be concerned with when you are improvising. While improvisation can be useful in dance performances, you should always be careful that your focus stays on God and only dancing from within and not for the purpose of showing off your ability. In times when you are dancing to be intimate with God, the last thing you need to be concerned about is how big that leap is or how high you can kick. God wants to see your heart, not your skill. He knows your ability and your talents. He gave them to you. God wants you to come and spend time alone with him so you can draw closer and deeper into a relationship with Him.

Learn It

Do you have a place where you can go to be alone and intimate with God? How often do you use this place?

How does it make you feel to know that God wants an intimate and personal relationship with you?

Have you ever used dance as a way to communicate personally with God? Why or why not?

Live It

Go somewhere you can be alone and pray. Take some time, at least a half an hour, to pray and talk to God through improvisation. It's okay if you don't know what to do. Just start moving and allow the Spirit to lead you. Allow yourself to shut out anything that is a distraction and focus on being intimate with God. Take note of any changes or new experiences in your heart, mind, or body.

Week 32

Choreography

Read It

Choreography is different from improvisation because the point of choreography is to be seen. It is created for the intention of communicating with an audience. God is still the biggest part of choreography, but it is not meant for only Him.

> *Matthew 10:19 – For it is not you who speak, but the Spirit of your Father speaking through you.*

If you allow God to be a part of your choreography, he will guide your steps and ideas. God wants the world to know the message of the gospel. Those who genuinely try to present his message will find that the Spirit leads them and makes the message clear for the recipients.

> *1 Corinthians 2:4 – And my speech and my message were not in plausible words of wisdom, but in demonstration of the Spirit and of power.*

Most people will not respond well to someone who tries to present the gospel like they are writing a doctorate level thesis on scripture. It will make Christianity seem intimidating and overwhelming. The gospel needs to be presented in a way that is relatable and comprehensible. Dance is a good platform for that kind of presentation. Dance can be a demonstration of the gospel by acting out the message or introducing ideas from scripture in a way that is visible and simple. Creating choreography that is not only visually appealing but also effectively communicative is a way to fulfill the need of a simple and reasonable presentation of the gospel.

> *Proverbs 4:26* – *Ponder the path of your feet; then all your ways will be sure.*

Choreography involves thinking and making decisions. Unlike improvisation, thinking and planning is the basis of choreography. You must make your decisions carefully so that the audience will grasp the concepts and messages you are trying to convey. As long as you consider carefully and allow the Spirit to drive your decisions, your message will be clear.

Choreography is an important part of Christian dance. It is the means to spreading God's word through an artistic channel. Being a choreographer is a big responsibility but it is also a gift from God.

Learn It

Everyone has different ways of choreographing. Do you have a particular way that you like best or find the easiest?

What can you do to prepare yourself to allow the Spirit to guide your choreography?

Why do you think it is important for the audience that you present your choreography in a way that is easy to understand?

Live It

Choose a story, idea, or message from scripture and
choreograph a brief dance about it. Choreograph it on
your own first; choosing movements you like and that
you think work well. Then choreograph it again but pray
about it and seek God's guidance. How does it change
what you have already done?

UPKEEP

OF A

CHRISTIAN

DANCER

Week 33

Body

Read It

*Christianity is almost the only one of the great religions
which thoroughly approves of the body – which believes that
matter is good, that God himself once took on a human
body, that some kind of body is going to be given to us even
in Heaven and is going to be an essential part of our
happiness, our beauty, and our energy.*
– C.S. Lewis

As a dancer, your body is your instrument of ministry.
Because of this, you must work to keep your body pure
and holy.

*1 Corinthians 3:16 – Do you not know that you are God's
temple and that God's spirit dwells in you?*

God lives in you. Just as you clean and prepare your
house for guests to arrive, you should also prepare your
body for God to dwell in it. Keep yourself pure and
physically able to carry out your gifts so that your temple,
your body, is always prepared for God.

*1 Corinthians 6:13 – "Food is meant for the stomach and
the stomach for food" – and God will destroy both one and
the other. The body is not meant for sexual immorality, but
for the Lord, and the Lord for the body.*

Your body was created for God. Your purpose is to use your body to bring God glory. Nothing else should rule the decisions you make with your body. If it does not please God, don't do it.

> *1 Thessalonians 4:3-5* – *For this is the will of God, your sanctification; that you abstain from sexual immorality; that each one of you know how to control his own body in holiness and honor, not in the passion of lust like the Gentiles who do not know God.*

Holiness and honor should be the aim of how we treat and present our bodies. God gave you a gift that uses your body. In order to give that back to him fully and use it for its true purpose, you must focus on keeping your body pure and honorable.

Maintaining your body for the fulfillment of your gift includes being physically active to keep your body able, being pure in your actions, and being outwardly honorable and modest.

Learn It

Why do you think it is so important to maintain your body?

What do you need to change or improve in order to keep your body pure and honorable and able?

If you find it difficult to maintain the purity of your body, what can you do to help keep that in check?

Live It

Make a fitness plan for yourself if you don't have one already. It is important for dancers to be physically healthy. Include someone in your plan who can keep you accountable and encourage your plan.

Make a list (you don't have to write it down) of ways that you struggle to stay pure. Find scripture that helps remind you to stay pure in these areas. If you need to, print or write them out and put them in the places you will need them most.

Week 34

Soul

Read It

Unity of your whole self includes unifying the body, soul, and spirit. The soul is the part of you that has emotion and desire. It is the part of you that either agrees or fights with your spirit, the reasoning side of you. It is what sets your body into action. Since you need to keep your body pure, you also need to keep your soul pure since it tends to dictate what your body does.

> *Psalm 24:3-4 – Who shall ascend the hill of the Lord? And who shall stand in his holy place? He who has clean hands and a pure heart, who does not lift up his soul to what is false and who does not swear deceitfully.*

The focus of your soul, or your heart, needs to be on what is true. God and his scripture are truth. If you ever doubt what your heart desires, see if it is in scripture. If it is, you are on track. If it is not, you need to reconsider where your focus is. This verse says that those with clean hands and pure hearts will stand in the holy place. This means those who are pure physically and pure emotionally. Your heart and your body need to align.

> *Matthew 5:8 – Blessed are the pure in heart, for they shall see God.*

The reward for having a pure heart is seeing God. This should be the number one desire of your soul. As long as you stay focused on God your heart will follow. Your heart expresses the true essence of who you are and is therefore the biggest identifier of your true purity.

> *1 Peter 1:22* – *Having purified your souls by your obedience to the truth for a sincere brotherly love, love one another earnestly from a pure heart.*

Purity of your soul is not just about having the right desires and emotions at the right time, but also about obeying the truth. It is knowing when your desires are pure and when they are not and obeying the call to be pure.

Purity of the soul produces purity of the body. You can keep your soul pure by focusing on truth and making the decision to obey the command of purity. When faced with temptations, your desires and emotions will be the first to get in the way. Keeping your desires in check with scripture and truth will allow you to make pure and holy decisions.

Learn It

Why is it important to make decisions slowly and carefully?

How can the decisions made from your desires and emotions affect decisions made with your body?

Why do you think it is important for a dancer to have a pure soul or heart?

Live It

As you are faced with decisions this week, big or small, take extra time to make sure your soul and your body align in purity. If you have a particularly difficult time keeping your desires or emotions reigned in about something, write it down, find applicable scripture, and pray about it before acting on anything.

Week 35

Spirit

Read It

Your spirit is the part of you that is rational and takes
responsibility. It is the decision making part of who you
are. This is the part of you that has the ability to turn
impure desires into pure decisions. Purity of spirit is the
cornerstone for having a pure soul and a pure body.

> *Romans 12:2 – Do not be conformed to this world, but be
> transformed by the renewal of your mind, that by testing you
> may discern what is the will of God, what is good and
> acceptable and perfect.*

A pure spirit starts with renewing your mind. It is easy to
make poor decisions if you do not know the truth of what
is right and wrong. Learning and knowing scripture is the
first step to understanding God's will in your decision
making. If you have a strong understanding of scripture
you will be able to determine good decisions quickly
when they come. It will become much easier to know
how to keep yourself pure.

> *Proverbs 15:28 – The heart of the righteous ponders how to
> answer, but the mouth of the wicked pours out evil things.*

This verse brings up a connection between the soul and
the spirit, the heart and the mind. The decisions of the
heart are based in the actions of the intellect. Making

decisions quickly and rashly can be very destructive to you and to others. A pure spirit understands the necessity to slow down, take time, and think before making any decisions. Taking the time to think can help you understand when you may be letting your emotions or desires steer you in the wrong direction.

> Philippians 4:8 – Finally, brothers, whatever is true, whatever is honorable, whatever is just, whatever is pure, whatever is lovely, whatever is commendable, if there is any excellence, if there is anything worthy of praise, think about these things.

Here you are advised to think about things that are pure and holy. If you keep your thoughts on things that are pleasing and acceptable to God, you will have a stronger rationale of truth and purity.

Being pure in spirit means you understand the importance of making decisions based on what you know to be true, not just what you feel. Having this purity in knowledge allows you to determine whether the emotions of your soul are pure, which will, in turn, decide the actions of your body.

Learn It

Do you ever have a struggle between what you know and what you feel? What is your normal process for decision making in these situations?

Why do you think it is important for a dancer to be able to make pure decisions consistently?

What can you do to help purify your spirit?

Live It

Learn a new scripture each day this week. Choose
scriptures that help you remember to slow down and
make pure decisions. Try to memorize these scriptures so
that when the time comes to make decisions, you will
have them engraved in your mind.

Week 36

Accountability

Read It

Accountability can be a scary thing. It is never fun to share with someone what makes you vulnerable and what your biggest temptations are, but it can be the best thing for your walk with God. Having someone you trust to help guide you and keep you accountable will help you grow in purity.

> _Galatians 6:1_ – _Brothers, if anyone is caught in any transgression, you who are spiritual should restore him in a spirit of gentleness. Keep watch on yourself, lest you too be tempted._

As Christians, it is our duty to look out for each other. If you see another Christian make a bad decision or do something you know is wrong, you should approach them. You do, however, need to be careful in how you do this. We are called to approach in a spirit of gentleness, not a spirit of judgment or blame. Christians need to help each other grow closer to Christ but they also need to grow closer to each other. In the same way, you need to watch your own decisions also.

> _Proverbs 27:17_ – _Iron sharpens iron, and one man sharpens another._

Accountability will hurt. It never feels good for someone

else to recognize when you have done something wrong and call you out on it, but it will make you a better, more knowledgeable Christian. It will help you learn from your mistakes and stand in purity. Do not be offended if someone sees your transgressions and confronts you about them. Feel honored that they care so much about your walk with God.

> *James 5:16* – *Therefore, confess your sins to one another and pray for one another, that you may be healed. The prayer of a righteous person has great power as it is working.*

It is important to talk to other Christians. It won't be easy, but it is necessary to have at least one other person who knows what your struggles are. You need someone who can talk to you and pray for you. You need someone who can encourage you and help you. And you need to do the same for other Christians. Fellowship and prayer are powerful tools for learning and understanding what God's will is for you.

Keeping yourself accountable is not an easy task but it is important. Christians are not only responsible for themselves, they are responsible for each other. We were made to have fellowship and that includes fellowship in accountability.

Learn It

What are some benefits of having someone who you can be accountable with and who can also be accountable with you?

Do you think you would make the same decisions if you consult with others instead of making decisions on your own?

What do you think is an appropriate way to approach someone you know is struggling with something or has already made a bad decision?

Live It

Find at least one other person this week who will agree to be an accountability partner with you (preferably someone who does not struggle with the same temptations you do). Agree to meet with this person(s) on a regular basis to discuss what you are struggling with, read scripture, and pray together.

BIBLICAL
EXAMPLES

Week 37

Miriam

Read It

Pulling one verse about dance from a longer story can sometimes hide some great details about the full meaning of dance in context. Because of this, it is important to look at examples of dance individually and view the significance in a greater scope of understanding.

Exodus 15 provides the first example of dance in the Bible. Reading the whole chapter is important to understand the context of why the Israelites were dancing here. In summary, this was just after the Israelites were freed from slavery in Egypt. They came to the Red Sea and, by the hand of God through Moses, were able to cross through the sea while the Egyptian army followed. God provided yet another escape from Egypt as the Israelites crossed and the Egyptians were swallowed by the sea. Below is the verse where the dancing begins.

> *Exodus 15:19-21 – For when the horses of Pharaoh with his chariots and his horsemen went into the sea, the Lord brought back the waters of the sea upon them, but the people of Israel walked on dry ground in the midst of the sea. Then Miriam the prophetess, the sister of Aaron, took a tambourine in her hand, and all the women went out after her with tambourines and dancing. And Miriam sang to them: "Sing to the Lord, for he has triumphed gloriously; the horse and his rider he has thrown into the sea."*

This verse is the first place where dance is mentioned. It is also the first place where Miriam's name is mentioned. She has been described as a prophetess, but she never had a major role in speaking. She did, however, begin the Israelite tradition of dancing in celebration. Miriam was the first leader whose skill in the arts was the ability she was known for. It was her medium for prophecy and her contribution to the worship style of the Israelites. She began the tradition of celebratory victory dancing.

> *It may appear strange that during so long an oppression in Egypt, the Israelites were able to cultivate the fine arts; but that they did so there is the utmost evidence from the Pentateuch. Not only architecture, weaving, and such necessary arts, were well known among them, but also the arts that are called ornamental, such as those of the goldsmith, lapidary, embroiderer, furrier, construction of the tabernacle and its utensils.*
> *-The Adam Clarke Commentary on Exodus 15*

The arts were a significant part of the life of the Israelites. Despite wandering in the desert for 40 years, God still gave them the ability to see and create beauty in the midst of a desolate and dry place. In a group of people who had to cry out just to survive and who had to trust God for their next day's meal, the arts were not just entertaining, they were necessary.

The great significance of dance in Exodus 15 is not just that it is a story of firsts, but that it is a story of beginnings.

Learn It

Why is this passage of scripture important for all Christian dancers?

When did your journey with dance begin? What made this beginning so significant for you?

Why do you think it is necessary for some leaders to be skilled in the arts? What benefit could that have for the people being led?

Live It

Read the chapters from Exodus about the escape from Egypt leading up to this celebration. Take notes on the events that caused such an outpouring of thanksgiving and celebration. Write down and reflect on some victories in your own life that you can celebrate with dance and singing.

Week 38

David

Read It

David is another prominent leader in the Old Testament and is probably the most famous dancer in the Bible. The great example of David dancing takes place after a series of successful endeavors led by King David. David had just recently been proclaimed King and had led the Israelites in taking over Jerusalem and conquering the Philistines. They were now bringing the Ark of the Covenant to its proper resting place in the City of David, Jerusalem.

> *2 Samuel 6:14-15 – And David danced before the Lord with all his might. And David was wearing a linen ephod. So David and all the house of Israel brought up the ark of the Lord with shouting and with the sound of the horn.*

There are several key points in this verse. First is that David danced with all his might. He gave everything he had to dance for God. Something that takes up this much of your energy and enthusiasm must be important. Dance is important as an expression of thanksgiving and praise. Another point is what David was wearing. An ephod is a priestly garment but not one to be worn alone. As Michal suggests in the next passage, David uncovered himself. This could mean that he was wearing only the ephod. In doing so, David would have been humbling himself before God while still showing the people that priests and kings are meant to celebrate and dance before God without being ashamed.

> *2 Samuel 6:20-23 – And David returned to bless his household. But Michal the daughter of Saul came out to meet David and said, "How the king of Israel honored himself today, uncovering himself today before the eyes of his servants' female servants, as one of the vulgar fellows shamelessly uncovers himself!" And David said to Michal, "It was before the Lord, who chose me above your father and above all his house, to appoint me as prince over Israel, the people of the Lord – and I will celebrate before the Lord. I will make myself yet more contemptible than this, and I will be abased in your eyes. But by the female servants of whom you have spoken, by them I shall be held in honor." And Michal the daughter of Saul had no child to the day of her death.*

Michal's response is the first sign of opposition to true Christian dance. The controversy over Christian dance is still strong today, but evidenced by God's punishment on Michal, dance is desired by God. He reacts harshly to those who oppose his people giving him praise. David stands firm in his decision to praise God, knowing that God is his true audience and no one can sway him from doing God's will.

Learn It

How natural is it for you to dance with all your might when you are praising God?

It is sometimes difficult to be humble while dancing in front of others. What do you do to stay focused on the reason you dance?

Do you face opposition to your decision to dance for Christ? What are the arguments against it and how should you respond?

Live It

Write down the reasons you dance. Think about these
often so that you are constantly reminded who dance is
for and how to respond to those who disagree with your
purpose.

Week 39

Jeremiah

Read It

Jeremiah 31 is describing God's promise to restore Israel. It is the promise of a New Covenant that will come through Jesus Christ. The promises are laced with joy and rejoicing which are expressed through song and dance.

> *Jeremiah 31:3-4 – I have loved you with an everlasting love; therefore I have continued my faithfulness to you. Again I will build you, and you shall be built, O virgin Israel! Again you shall adorn yourself with tambourines and shall go forth in the dance of the merrymakers.*

This verse is an exciting proclamation. God gives us so much to be joyful about. After hearing about his eternal love, unending faithfulness, and promise of restoration, you should be so excited that you can't help but dance. And the wonderful part is that these promises are constant. They never change and never fail, so you should rejoice all the time knowing that God always loves you and cares for you this much.

> *Jeremiah 31:13 – Then shall the young women rejoice in the dance, and the young men and old shall be merry. I will turn their mourning into joy; I will comfort them, and give them gladness for sorrow.*

This verse contrasts the emotions of the old and the new. With the outcomes of the new promises, the promise of restoration and a savior, come rejoicing and joy and gladness expressed through dance. Dance is the antonym of sorrow.

The scriptures in Jeremiah 31 give a hope for God's promises. They give a reason to be in constant joy. Even if the good times and restoration have not come yet, God has promised them to you and that should at least bring peace and joy to your heart. But the result of the promise will be a joy that cannot be contained. It will be an overflowing joy that has to find an external outlet. Dance is visible, moving joy.

Learn It

Can you think of a time in your life when you have had a bad circumstance restored to something good? What was your reaction when you knew the tides would turn?

Why do you think dance is a good way to express joy in restoration?

How are expressions of joy different from expressions of mourning? Can you use dance to express both emotions?

Live It

Read Jeremiah 31. Think of a time in your life when you have gone through a difficult or trying time. This may be something that happened to you or even a time when you turned away from God. Think about the emotions during the hard time and contrast them with the outcome. The joy of coming through the difficulties should be greater than the weight of the sorrow. If it isn't, read Jeremiah 31 again. Write down the reasons you have to rejoice in God's restoration. Dance for joy in God's presence.

Week 40

Prodigal Son

Read It

The story of the Prodigal Son is one of great celebration. The story goes that a son asked for his inheritance early, left the father's house and spent all of his money until he had no money, no job, and no home. The son came home after a long time, expecting the father to be disappointed and angry, but instead the father rejoiced that his long lost son was alive and home. He celebrated his return.

> *Luke 15:25-27 – Now his older son was in the field, and as he came and drew near to the house, he heard music and dancing. And he called one of the servants and asked what these things meant. And he said to him, "Your brother has come, and your father has killed the fattened calf, because he has received him back safe and sound."*

In this story dancing is used to celebrate someone who has been lost returning home. For dancers now, that could mean celebrating a person who was lost and has come to Christ. Dance is a great expression of rejoicing and what better event is there to rejoice about than the eternal salvation of a new believer?

> *Luke 15:32 – It was fitting to celebrate and be glad, for this your brother was dead, and is alive; he was lost, and is found.*

The older brother of this parable was angry and jealous that the father celebrated the return of a brother who was so careless and who had previously abandoned the family. He thought that he should have a reward for his faithfulness. This verse was the father's response. What the older brother didn't realize is that the celebration was more about the forgiveness that the younger brother sought after than what his actions may have been.

The reward for a Christian is in Heaven. You should not expect glory and fairness in your earthly life. That does not mean that you can't join in the celebration though. Christians have a lot to celebrate and one of those is every new believer who becomes a part of the body of Christ and, therefore, part of your family. Rejoice in the lost who are found. Celebrate with the rest of the body of Christ and give what you have: dance.

Learn It

Why do you think it is important to make the lost feel welcome and to celebrate their decision to come to Christ?

What was the last thing you celebrated with dance? Why were you celebrating?

What are some other major events that you can celebrate with other believers using dance?

Live It

Think of some major events that would encourage celebration. Decide on at least one that you would like to celebrate with dance. Even if you don't want to do it with the whole church, at least get a few other dancers to join you and either choreograph or freely worship on the day of that event. You may want to ask your pastor and worship director if you can dance at these events to lead the church in rejoicing also (maybe Christmas, Easter, a baptism service, etc.)

Herodias' Daughter

Read It

The example of Herodias' daughter dancing is an example of unholy dance. While dance was created by and for God, it has since been corrupted and used wrongly in countless ways. In this example dance is used for personal gain.

King Herod had been keeping John the Baptist in prison at the time. Herod did not like John the Baptist because he had disapproved of Herod for an inappropriate relationship he was having. He wanted to kill John the Baptist, but was afraid to because he knew the people he ruled held John in high regard. This passage comes in the context of a birthday celebration for Herod.

> *Matthew 14:5-11 – And though he (Herod) wanted to put him (John the Baptist) to death, he feared the people, because they held him to be a prophet. But when Herod's birthday came, the daughter of Herodias danced before the company and pleased Herod, so that he promised with an oath to give her whatever she might ask. Prompted by her mother, she said, "Give me the head of John the Baptist here on a platter." And the king was sorry, but because of his oaths and his guests he commanded it to be given. He sent and had John beheaded in the prison, and his head was brought on a platter and given to the girl, and she brought it to her mother.*

In this example, dance was used as a tool for selfish gain. Herodias' daughter danced in a way that was pleasing and probably seductive to King Herod. He became so entranced by watching her body that he let his guard down and made a foolish promise. Dance is powerful and if used for the wrong purposes it can have tragic and foolish outcomes. The source of corruption in this story was the selfishness that motivated the actions of Herodias and her daughter. Dance that is created from a corrupt heart will result in a corrupt performance and audience.

> _Mark 6:20_ – _For Herod feared John, knowing that he was a righteous and holy man, and he kept him safe. When he heard him, he was greatly perplexed, and yet he heard him gladly._

This verse is a little bit of background information on the relationship between King Herod and John the Baptist. Herod actually had a level of respect for John, knowing that he was good and holy. He enjoyed John's preaching, but still became the person responsible for his death.

This example of dance is a clear demonstration of why it is important to keep your body, soul, and spirit in unity with the purpose of dance. Always stay focused on God and doing his will through dance. The results of your performance are directly affected by the source of your motivation.

Learn It

Why do you think Herod was so easily swayed?

How powerful do you think the effect of dance is on an audience? Can it stir up emotions and ideas?

In what ways can you make sure to keep yourself from allowing corruption to enter your heart and mind while dancing?

Live It

Find scripture about character. Write down any verses that are particularly helpful to something you struggle with. Pray about and study these scriptures. Remind yourself of them anytime you dance.

Week 42

Revelation

Read It

A wonderful thing about having the gift of eternal life is that you also get the gift of eternal praise. The gifts and talents that God gives are not just for here on Earth. You get to dance and praise God forever. The examples of worship in Revelation are a beautiful picture of how dance will be used in eternity.

> *Revelation 19:4-5 - And the twenty-four elders and the four living creatures fell down and worshiped God who was seated on the throne, saying, "Amen. Hallelujah!" And from the throne came a voice saying, "Praise our God, all you his servants, you who fear him, small and great."*

The Greek word for worship that is used in this verse actually means to prostrate oneself, to bow down, or to kiss the ground. Even in Heaven you will be praising God with the posture of your body. Your movements have great meaning and you get to use your body and your words to praise God for eternity. Dance and movement will be an important form of worship in Heaven!

> *Revelation 19:7 – Let us rejoice and exult and give him the glory, for the marriage of the Lamb has come, and his Bride has made herself ready.*

In Heaven, you will get to be a part of the biggest and greatest marriage ceremony ever. That calls for the best celebration too! Since it has always been appropriate to celebrate with song and dance, how amazing will the celebration of the Lamb and his Bride be? You will get to dance as you never imagined possible on Earth and it will be for your marriage to Christ!

> *Revelation 22:3* – *No longer will there be anything accursed, but the throne of God and of the Lamb will be in it, and his servants will worship him.*

The word 'accursed' in this scripture means 'something devoted to destruction.' That means that nothing that God created will be corrupt in Heaven. It will be restored to its original purpose and purity. That means that in Heaven you can dance without hindrance. There will be no one to question whether it is okay or tell you that dance is sin. You will be free to use your gift in the most beautiful, pure, and holy way that God intended for it to be used.

Dance in Revelation is dance of worship and celebration and freedom. It is a celebration of the culmination of God's sacrifice and love. You get to bring your gift with you and use it to praise God for eternity.

Learn It

What are you most looking forward to about Heaven?

What do you think it will be like to dance in Heaven?

How can the knowledge that you will dance in Heaven affect the way you dance now?

Live It

Find scripture about worship in Heaven. Using what you learn from these scriptures, write down how you think dance will be used in Heaven. Compare what you think the similarities and differences are in dance as worship in Earth and Heaven.

DANCE AND THE HISTORY OF THE CHURCH

Week 43

Old Testament

Read It

Throughout the history of Christianity dance has gone through periods of acceptance, controversy, and complete intolerance. To understand the role of dance presently and for the future of the Christian church, a brief look at the history of dance is necessary. Let's start at the very beginning.

613 – This is the number of laws that are laid out in the first five books of the Old Testament.

The 613 laws or commandments found in the Old Testament are known as the Mosaic Law. These laws give very specific regulations for everything from religious celebrations to moral obligations. There are laws for everything from the very obvious down to the very particular about what you can eat and how you must do your hair. In recognizing how specific these laws are, it would be rational to say that if there was something God did not approve of, there would be a law about it. There is no law anywhere in scripture saying that any form of dance is not acceptable.

44 – This is the number of Hebrew words there are for dance.

Not all of these Hebrew words are used in scripture, but

quite a few are and the language of the culture of the Old Testament was Hebrew. For one English word to be expressed 44 different ways in the language of the Old Testament means that the true meaning of dance has probably been diminished through translation and cultural differences. You know that dance was commonly used for praise, worship, festivals, and ceremonies in the Old Testament and that there were several examples of dance being used in appropriate and edifying ways. What is probably lost to those who don't know Hebrew well is the difference in meaning from one word for dance to another. Just as in English you can say 'he ran', 'he jogged', or 'he sprinted' all to mean that this person was travelling faster than a walk, these different Hebrew words for dance probably gave more indication of the purpose and intensity behind the action.

Dance was a common practice for Israelites. They used dance in their everyday lives as well as at celebrations like weddings and at festivals such as the Feast of Tabernacles. Dance served many purposes and was an unquestionable part of the lives of those who loved and served God.

Learn It

Why do you think it is important to know the history of
dance in the church?

What can dance in the Old Testament teach you about
what dance should look like in the church today and in
the future?

Why do you think there was little controversy about
dance during the times of the Old Testament?

Live It

Research two different festivals or celebrations that were common for the Israelites during the Old Testament. Find out what the role of dance was in those celebrations. Think about what the festival meant, what it was honoring, and how dance represented the purpose.

Week 44

New Testament

Read It

There are not as many references to dance in the New Testament as there are in the Old Testament. Because of this, several different opinions have arisen about whether dance was still considered holy.

Some believe that because New Testament scripture does not mention dance very much in example and is never directly taught by Jesus that it is not an acceptable form of worship. This may seem logical if you only look for the actual word "dance." However, the words 'trinity' and 'rapture' cannot be found anywhere in scripture, but the concepts are widely accepted in the Christian faith. There are examples of people throughout the New Testament who leapt with joy or rejoiced greatly after being healed or seeing Jesus. Some prime examples of this are when John the Baptist leapt in the womb at the presence of Jesus when Mary approached (Luke 1:41) or when the beggar at the temple was healed and jumped up to praise God (Acts 3:8) or when Jesus commands those who are persecuted to rejoice and leap for joy (Luke 6:23).

The people of this time period would be accustomed to the tradition of dance as a form of worship and celebration so it is likely that dancing still happened just as often as it did in the Old Testament but that it just did not need to be taught as an accepted practice. There is also less mention in the New Testament of musical instruments and singing but there is no question that those are still wonderful ways to praise God.

The places that do mention dance specifically refer to dance with a driving force and passion. There is a strong purpose behind the dance and that is a basis for believing that dance is the result of an intense need for worship, praise, celebration. In the example of the Prodigal Son in Luke 15, the father explains that there is every reason to celebrate in that situation. Dance is expected of such a joyous occasion. In Matthew 11:17 a generation who rejects Christ is compared to people who do not dance at the sound of music. Dancing in this verse is symbolic of the desired response to God's call. God has invited you to be his forever. Get up and dance!

The New Testament is also where the connection between body, soul, and spirit becomes clear. As a triune God is revealed in the New Testament, so is the triune self. You were created in the image of God, complete with the unity of these three parts. You are told in 1 Corinthians 3:16 that your body is the temple of God. The temple is the place where people pray and worship God and the place where God dwells.

While dance is not as prominently mentioned in the New Testament, it still has God's approval. He desires his people to rejoice, to celebrate, and to dance.

Learn It

Why do you dance?

When you are overcome with joy, how do you express yourself?

How can you be sure that your body, soul, and spirit are working together when you worship?

Live It

Find a few examples of people rejoicing in the New Testament. Write down what you think their physical reaction would have been if you saw the circumstance played out.

Early Church

Read It

Job 8:8 – *For inquire, please, of bygone ages, and consider what the fathers have searched out.*

In the very early church, dance was part of the traditional liturgy. In two of the earliest Christian liturgies recorded, dance was an element of the service. Several church fathers have written about how simple and traditional dance movements were used during services and the role that dance played as a form of worship. At this point, dance was still a very widely accepted form of worship in Christianity.

The Lord bids us dance, not merely with the circling movements of the body, but with the pious faith in him.
-Ambrose (AD 340-397)

As more people converted to Christianity, dance faced the beginnings of a downfall. The people who converted tried to maintain some of their pagan dance forms which focused the attention of dance on the movement of the body rather than the meaning of the action. Many of the church fathers during this time, including Ambrose, encouraged Christians to remember and return to the spiritual motivation and purpose of dance. Other church fathers argued that dance was evil and should be removed from church services. A conflict began and in some places, dance was removed entirely from churches, others only allowed bishops and elders to dance, and in other places dance was closely monitored for signs of corruption. The result of this division was a steady decline in the presence of dance in the church.

During the Renaissance era, books began to be printed and an emphasis shifted to the intellect rather than the body. The mind was given preference and in this era the only dance that survived was highly ritualized and literal for the purpose of acting out or explaining. The focus of Christianity and culture changed from acting out one's faith to studying and praying in quiet, making knowledge the center of faith.

> *The heathen are the inventors of dance.*
> *-Excerpt from a Reformation (1517-1529) booklet printed in Utrecht, the center of Christianity in the Netherlands*

The Reformation era brought the most change for dance. This era was marked by a dedication for suppressing icons and dance was seen as glorifying the body. Dance and other performing and visual arts were considered frivolous and unnecessary to the Christian faith. Despite several church leaders such as Martin Luther and William Tyndale supporting dance, dance almost completely disappeared in churches in the Reformation, only surviving in a few denominations.

Learn It

How does culture affect worship?

Why do you think it important to heed the advice of Job 8:8?

Has anyone ever tried to tell you that dance is sinful? How did you or would you respond?

Live It

Take time this week to reflect on your journey with dance. Write down ways that you incorporate culture into your praise dance. Determine how you find the line between influencing culture and being influenced by culture.

Week 46

Present Church

Read It

Dance in the church today has become much more diverse and vibrant since the time of the Reformation when dance was almost completely eradicated. Dance as a form of worship is found in many nations, cultures, and denominations, but still is not accepted by everyone of Christian faith.

There are a few reasons that dance is not completely accepted in the church today. One is that dance has been so perverted and corrupted that it is difficult to still see it as something that can glorify God. Dance is used to sell things. Dance is used to show off. Dance is used to seduce. None of these purposes came from God. None of them fulfill the purpose of dance in scripture. But Satan cannot create, he can only copy. That means that while dance has been corrupted in the world, there is a holy and original purpose for dance that still exists. In order to revive dance in the church, a very distinct separation needs to be clear between worldly dance and holy Christian dance. Worldly dance has perverted God's purpose for dance and does not reflect his character. Holy Christian dance fulfills a call to lead worship and spread God's word. God has entrusted his people with this gift. It is the dancers' duty to represent God well by using what he has given.

Another reason dance is not completely accepted is because many churches follow the same traditional patterns they have had since their denomination was created. Since dance is not part of their church already, it does not seem important to pursue inclusion of dance in services. The problem here is getting stuck in a rut and allowing the wisdom of the church fathers to outweigh the wisdom of scripture. If you are in a church like this and have no outlet to use your gift, it may be time to step up and talk to your pastor or worship leader. There is nothing wrong with asking why and that may be a good place to start.

In the face of these problems for dance in the church, dancers across the globe have risen to their call. In addition to the spread of its acceptance in church services and as a ministry, there are also professional dance companies that seek to spread God's word nationally and globally, as well as Christian dance guilds and organizations that seek to connect dancers across the world. This renewal of dance is the beginning of a full restoration. It is a light to guide you and other Christian dancers to fulfill the purpose God has and work toward the restitution of dance as a fully accepted form of worship.

It is up to you as a dancer to be a tool for restoration and for making the original purpose of dance the most recognized purpose. Despite the controversy of dance, it has begun to spread through the church. The only reason this has happened is because more and more dancers just like you are responding to the call and taking it seriously.

Learn It

What are some ways that you have seen dance corrupted?
What do you think is the source of this corruption?

Have you been or are you part of a church that does not
accept dance? What can you do to help make the purpose
of dance known?

Live It

As you watch TV this week, take note of how often you see dance in commercials and TV shows. What is it being used for?

Find a couple of Christian dance companies, ministries, or organizations. Write down who they are and what their mission/vision is for dance. Do they align and what do they base their mission on in scripture?

Week 47

Future Church

Read It

The future church is in Heaven. It is the place and time when everything that God has created will be restored to its original purpose. God's people will worship him as one body for eternity.

> _Acts 3:19-21_ – _Repent therefore, and turn again, that your sins may be blotted out, that times of refreshing may come from the presence of the Lord, and that he may send the Christ appointed for you, Jesus, whom heaven must receive until the time for restoring all things about which God spoke by the mouth of his holy prophets long ago._

This message is referring to the time when Christ comes again to take his people to Heaven. Jesus is in Heaven now awaiting the time of restoration. The word "restoring" here means to return to a more perfect state. Since it refers to all things spoken by prophets it means that this is everything written in scripture returned to the way God created it. That includes worship and dance being returned to a pure and holy act. There will no longer be any defilement in the act of dance or any reason to think it unworthy of being presented to God.

> _Philippians 3:20-21_ – _But our citizenship is in heaven, and from it we await a Savior, the Lord Jesus Christ, who will transform our lowly body to be like his glorious body, by the_

power that enables him even to subject all things to himself.

Every person in Heaven will receive a new heavenly body. According to this scripture it will be like the body of Christ. No one really knows what this means exactly but it will be much more capable than the physical, earthly bodies of the present. You may be able to do things you could not even dream of here. You will not grow weary or run out of breath when you dance. You will be able to worship to your fullest.

> *Revelation 5:13 – And I heard every creature in heaven and on earth and under the earth and in the sea, and all that is in them, saying, "To him who sits on the throne and to the Lamb be blessing and honor and glory and might forever and ever!"*

The reason God created humankind was to worship and glorify him. That is the privilege of being one of his children. You get to worship him for eternity in Heaven with all the creatures of the Earth and Heaven! You have the honor of coming together with men and women, angels, and all the creatures of Earth to worship him forever! With that mix of worshipers there is sure to be dancing, singing, music, and other forms of worship mere humans probably could not even conceive.

Learn It

How different do you think worship will be once everything is restored to its original created state?

What do you think you will be able to do with a Heavenly body that you cannot do now? How will this change how you worship through dance?

Imagine a worship service including people from every country as well as angels and creatures of the earth and sea. What do you think that worship would look like?

Live It

Each time you dance this week, remember the hope for restoration, a heavenly body, and eternal worship. Allow the thoughts of this worship in the future church to guide your attitude and prayers in dance classes, on stage, and in your everyday life outside of dance. Remember that you will be a dancer for Christ for eternity, not just here on Earth. Your heart should reflect this eternal desire when using your gift.

DANCE
AND
EVANGELISM

Week 48

The Church and Ministry

Read It

Having different ministries in a church allows each member to give who they are for the purpose of reaching people in every way possible. Everyone has different gifts and talents and if they are not being used to benefit the body of Christ and spread God's word, then they are not being used properly. Every gift and talent that God has given needs an outlet for expression.

> *1 Corinthians 7:17* – *Only let each person lead the life that the Lord has assigned to him, and to which God has called him. This is my rule in all the churches.*

God is the only one who can decide what your gifts and talents are. His rule for the church is that each person has a way to use those gifts. This is why each church has different ministries. Some are called to teach children, others are talented musicians; some have a knack for drama, while some may be great youth pastors. The relationship between the church and its ministries begins with the church giving an opportunity for each person to follow God's call on his or her life.

> *1 Corinthians 14:12* – *So with yourselves, since you are eager for manifestations of the Spirit, strive to excel in building up the church.*

Once the church has made it possible for a person or group to have a ministry, the ministry needs to do its part. The goal of a ministry should be to share the love of God and build up the church. If there is a conflict between your ministry and the leaders of the church or even one person in the ministry and one leader of the church, that conflict must be resolved before the ministry can fulfill its purpose. The people in the church and its ministries make up the church body. That body needs to be in unity.

> Romans 12:4-5 – For as in one body we have many members, and the members do not all have the same function, so we, though many, are one body in Christ, and individually members one of another.

God has given everyone different talents for a reason. If all Christians had the same gifts and personalities, it would be very difficult to reach people. For this reason, he has laid different callings on each person's life and as you fulfill yours, you are becoming a part of the body of Christ. You are making it complete. As a body, it is important to stay unified and focused on the true purpose of the gifts God has given.

The church is a foundation for ministry. A church is unified by a vision or mission statement and the ministries involved in the church need to abide by the calling of the church as well as the calling God has placed on the lives of those involved. The church gives to the ministry by finding an outlet for the talents in the church. The ministry gives to the church by edifying the members and reaching out to the community.

Learn It

Does your church have an outlet for a dance ministry? If not, why do you think that is?

How could you approach a leader in your church to request permission to start a dance ministry?

As a dancer or member of a dance ministry, in what ways can you be supportive of your church while edifying the members and the community?

Live It

Pray for your church leaders and the ministries in your church this week. Pray that the church will remember their purpose for ministry and will be accepting of all members of the body of Christ. Pray that the ministries will fully embrace the vision of the church and work in one accord with its leaders to fulfill the purpose God has for them.

Week 49

The Ministry and the Dancers

Read It

Ministries benefit more than just the church and the congregation. They benefit the people involved also. Likewise, dance ministries are not only good for the audience who is affected by the dance, but also the dancers who are affected by the learning experience and the process of sharing God's word through the gifts he has given.

> *Psalm 87:7 – Singers and dancers alike say, "All my springs are in you."*

It is important to remember from where your gifts come. A spring is a source of water, a source of life. The singers and dancers in this psalm have recognized that God is their source of life. He gives them everything they need, including the talents of music and dance.

> *1 Corinthians 6:20 – Glorify God in your body.*

By glorifying God with your body, you should not only be an example for those who see you, but also to yourself. Anytime you glorify God with your whole self you are giving your life to him again. In a dance ministry, you are constantly reminded of this purpose behind what you do. Use this reminder to get closer to God and become fully engaged in your worship. Use it to build up your relationship.

> *Proverbs 9:9 – Give instruction to a wise man, and he will be still wiser; teach a righteous man, and he will increase in learning.*

The beauty in teaching is that it is never just the student who learns. Those who are instructed by someone who is founded in Christ and lives his or her purpose will be wiser and grow in their relationship with God. That teaching will be a foundation for their knowledge of Christ. In order for the student to learn in such a way, the teacher must be constantly searching and learning also. It is the duty of the teacher to be prepared and to be completely devoted to his or her relationship with God in order to instruct others.

Dance is a powerful gift. It touches the lives of everyone involved, not just everyone who sees. It brings understanding and builds up relationships. It is a physical and visible reminder of your faith. Allow dance to be not just an external learning experience and presentation of what you know, but also an internal growing experience and representation of who you are.

Learn It

How have you benefited in your walk with God through dance?

Is there a person (teacher, choreographer, etc) in your dance journey who has affected your relationship with God? How?

Do you think the audience and body of the church will be more affected by your dance if you are also affected by dance? Why or why not?

Live It

Whenever you dance this week, keep your heart and mind in tune with what your body is doing. Focus on what the movements mean, not just on what they look like. Read scripture and pray every day. Keep yourself close to God so that you will be the most effective tool for his purpose that you can be.

Week 50

Dancers and the Audience

Read It

I see dance being used as communication between body and soul, to express what is too deep, too fine for words.
- Ruth St. Denis

Dance is more than just pleasing to the eye. It has a purpose and a driving force. It has a message to send. Dance can communicate ideas and stories. It can help the audience have a clearer understand of God's message in scripture. This way of communicating can bridge gaps for people who learn differently or just need to see in order to understand. It can help reach people who may not be reachable otherwise. Many people who are closed off to hearing God's word may be more accepting of just watching a dance. It could help those who do understand God's love know deeper, and it can help those who do not understand God's love have the opportunity to see the beauty of it and ask questions or be willing to hear.

Matthew 13:34 – All these things Jesus said to the crowds in parables; indeed, he said nothing to them without a parable.

Parables were stories that explained what Jesus was really trying to say in a way that the people would be able to see and understand. In the same way, dance allows the scripture to come to life and be visible. Hearing the word plants the seed of understanding, but seeing it and relating to it makes it grow into a beautiful relationship with Christ. Dance as a visual, non-verbal form of communication allows the audience to see scripture. It is an especially helpful tool in communicating to people who are more visual learners as well as people who may not speak the same language or are difficult to communicate with verbally.

> *1 John 3:18* – *Little children, let us not love in word or talk but in deed and in truth.*

Your actions show what you truly care about. When you teach scripture through dance you are able to visually pour out your love for God and your love for people. Using your gifts for the purpose of bringing people closer to their Creator is an act of love. This means guiding the audience in truth through the message of your dance.

In order for dance to be a tool for communication, it must represent the word of God. It must be founded in truth and love with a goal of bringing understanding. Dance is powerful so it is important to be vigilant about communicating truth and love.

Learn It

Why do you think dance is an important way to communicate God's love?

Who do you think would benefit most from dance as a way of communicating?

What are some messages that would be significant to tell through dance?

Live It

Think of one or two stories or messages in scripture that convey God's love or tell about salvation. Choose appropriate music and try to give the message through dance. Show it to someone and see if they understand the message through what they see. Take notes on what was most clearly understood by your audience and what didn't make sense.

Pray for your audience this week. Even if you are not performing in front of anyone soon, just remember that when you dance it is for their understanding and for God's glory. Pray that anyone who sees you dance will have an open heart and a clear mind, ready to accept the message that God sends through you.

Week 51

Dance and Other Ministries

Read It

Dance, as with all ministries, does not act alone. There are other ministries that feed into the dance ministry and benefit from it also. These ministries most commonly include the music and drama ministry, but the dance ministry is also affected by the preaching as well as anyone behind the scenes, like the light and sound operators. It is hard to come by a passage of scripture about dance that does not include another ministry.

> *Psalm 149:1-3 – Praise the Lord! Sing to the Lord a new song, his praise in the assembly of the godly! Let Israel be glad in his Maker; let the children of Zion rejoice in their King! Let them praise his name with dancing, making melody to him with tambourine and lyre!*

This scripture, like many others where dance is present, includes dancing, singing, and musical instruments. It is the combination of these that makes pleasing praise. One of these alone is still praise, but when your gift is combined with others it brings a fullness and sweetness to the sound and sight.

> *Acts 4:32 – Now the full number of those who believed were of one heart and soul, and no one said that any of the things that belonged to him was his own, but they had everything in common.*

The gift of dance is not meant to be kept to yourself or used only for your benefit. This scripture refers to a time when the disciples and believers came together to provide the needs for those around them. Whatever they had, they gave to those who needed it. That is what you should do with the gifts God has given you. This can be achieved by working together in unity with other ministries. By bringing multiple ministries together to serve people in the name of God, you are participating in a powerful movement of love and service. You are being of "one heart and soul" with believers who have complementary talents and gifts.

> *1 Corinthians 12:17* – *If the whole body were an eye, where would be the sense of hearing? If the whole body were an ear, where would be the sense of smell?*

The context of this verse is when the body of Christ is being compared to a physical body. The message here is that we need each other's gifts and talents to be a complete representation of the body of Christ. Working together for the goal of glorifying God and spreading his word unifies the body of Christ.

Being in unity with other ministries is not just a message to people who are affected by the ministries; it is also a message to the members of the ministries. The message you send to other ministries by eagerly participating in worship with them is that you understand the worth of their gift and the importance of your union. You build each other up in encouragement and love by working together and acknowledging the differences in your talents through the unity of your purpose.

Learn It

What other ministries at your church would work well with a dance ministry?

Are there any ministries that are not commonly linked to dance that could be partnered with the dance ministry for a unique affiliation?

What can you do to support other ministries in your church?

Live It

Pray for the other ministries in your church this week. Ask God to give you the opportunities to join with them and combine your gifts to bring God deeper worship.

Seek out opportunities to join with the other ministries of your church. This could be dancing with live music or a choir or even having the members of the drama team participate in your dance or vice versa.

Week 52

Global Dance

Read It

When we worship as we ought that's when the nations listen.
– Edmund Clowney

The Great Commission calls all of God's people to spread God's word throughout the Earth. This doesn't mean that everyone has to go to foreign countries and learn the language and minister to people across the globe. But it does mean that everyone has to participate in the effort to make God's word known to everyone. Some may be called to other countries. Some may be called to other cities. Others may be called to be prayer warriors or financial supporters. Everyone has a part, including dancers.

> *Isaiah 52:7 – How beautiful upon the mountains are the feet of him who brings good news, who publishes peace, who brings good news of happiness, who publishes salvation, who says to Zion, "Your God reigns."*

God delights in those who spread his word. Evangelism is not confined to people who have the ability to preach and teach. This verse does not say "how beautiful are the feet of those who preach." It is about anyone who brings good news. Dancers are part of that group! There are many dancers who travel the world in a performance group or as part of a mission organization. Dance is a universal language. You don't need a translator to make people understand your message. It is a powerful tool of communication for anyone, not just people you are familiar with or who know your language or customs. People everywhere dance. You have the ability to spread God's word in a way that can already be understood by everyone in the world!

> *Matthew 24:14 – And this gospel of the kingdom will be proclaimed throughout the whole world as a testimony to all nations, and then the end will come.*

Many nations do not allow the gospel to be preached within their borders. However, many of these nations will allow people to come in as artists, teaching dance, art, or drama. Coming to those places as a dance teacher or even drama instructor allows a new avenue for sharing the gospel. It helps break into a place where God's word may have gone unheard or unsupported. It allows his love and grace to penetrate an unreachable place.

> *Revelation 15:4 – Who will not fear, O Lord, and glorify your name? For you alone are holy. All nations will come and worship you, for your righteous acts have been revealed.*

This glimpse of worship in Heaven is a great reminder that the world will come together and worship God as one in the future church. Why not start that relationship now? It is important for the body of Christ to extend past a single church, a single town, a single country. The body of Christ is in the whole world and it is the duty of believers to make that body bigger so that more people can join in worshipping God in Heaven.

Learn It

How can dance speak to people who don't understand the same language?

Why is it important for Christian dance to be spread across the globe?

What can you do to be a part of the global movement of dancing for God?

Live It

Remember that the goal of any ministry is to seek out the lost and spread God's word. Pray for the lost souls all over the world. Even if you cannot go to the ends of the Earth, pray for the opportunity to partner with or just connect with missionaries.

Look up one or two dance ministries that travel globally. Send them a message of encouragement and prayer. Let them know that they are supported and loved by people who understand their ministry and the impact it has on God's kingdom.

Made in the USA
Monee, IL
13 November 2020

47505083R00128